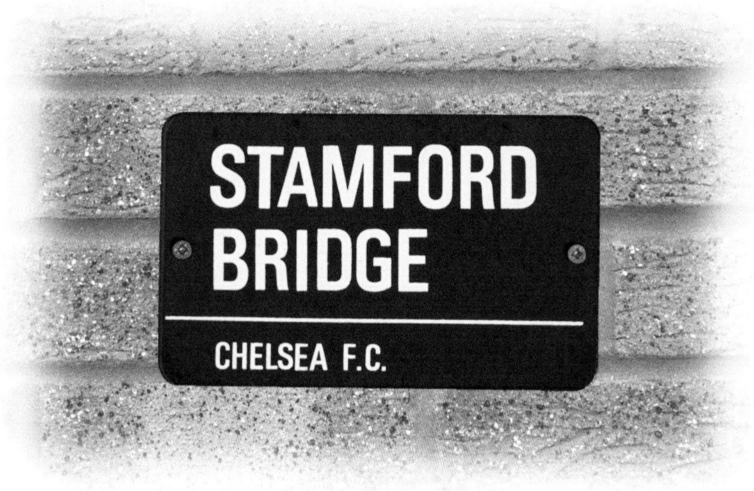
STAMFORD
BRIDGE
CHELSEA F.C.

# Blue is the Colour

by Khadija Buckland

Sponsored by Coors®

A Red House Publication
ISBN 0 9522519 2 2

## AUTHOR'S ACKNOWLEDGEMENTS

Blue is the Colour is now a reality but for many years it has been a dream for me.

It all started when I was a child and saw the FA Cup come to Stamford Bridge in 1970, held aloft by the players as the open-top bus made its way through the crowds. What a celebration! I knew I would never forget that moment.

As I got older I was determined to chronicle that very special era in Chelsea's history.

What better time than on the silver anniversary, especially as the Club is now on the verge of even more exciting times ahead.

This book has also brought me back to my roots in Chelsea. The present and future, are, after all, only possible because of the past.

Blue is the Colour is only a reality because of Chelsea, the staff and players both past and present. Without their contribution and the Club's official endorsement, the book would have remained a dream.

Special thanks to everyone at Chelsea: in particular Ken Bates, Matthew Harding, Colin Hutchinson, Glenn Hoddle and Carole Phair.

Thanks also to the 1970s squad, in particular Peter Osgood who put me in touch with all the players.

And to William Younger, including: Managing Director Charles Williamson, Commercial Director Ian Copeland, PR and Events Manager Ben Gibson and Coors Brand Manager Michael Jarvis. Without their sponsorship, the book would not have been of such high quality.

Special thanks also to Robin Alexander, Managing Director – Take Home Sales Scottish Courage Ltd.

Also to Action Images whose brilliant photography brings the book to life and to statsman Ron Hockings.

Thanks also to Robert for his editing skills as well as never-ending patience, Jon Ellis, Paul Ridgewell, Corey Ross and to all Chelsea fans everywhere.

Photographs courtesy of , Sir Richard Attenborough, George Anstiss, Eddie Barnett, Chelsea Football Club, Ron Harris, Ron Hockings, Ian Jenkins and Special Events Photography.

Efforts have been made to trace copyright holders of all photographs used in this book. We apologise for any omissions, which are unintentional and would be pleased to include an appropriate acknowledgement in any subsequent edition.

Statistics courtesy of Ron Hockings, author of *Ninety Years of The Blues – a statistical history, 1905 -1995*.

Printed by Acorn Press Swindon Limited — ACORN PRESS SWINDON LIMITED

Blue is the Colour is dedicated to George Anstiss, Chelsea's former head groundsman, who died earlier this year before this book's publication. George was the ultimate Chelsea fan – the Club was his life.

# CONTENTS

Introduction by Ken Bates.

# INTRODUCTION

WELCOME to Blue is the Colour - a book which officially celebrates the 25th anniversary of a glorious chapter in Chelsea's history.

All fans of the Blues who are old enough to remember the remarkable 1970 Cup Final and replay will relive the agony and ecstasy of that time.

Those who are too young will now understand why it warrants such an important place in the Blues legend.

But Blue is the Colour is more than just a look back at the events of 25 years ago. It also celebrates our more recent successes in the European Cup Winners' Cup, charts the history of the Club from its very beginnings and comes bang up to date with our summer super-signings.

I have been Chairman of Chelsea for 13 years now and I have never known such a buzz of excitement about the Club.

There is a feeling that Chelsea really are on the brink of the success that has eluded us for too long.

There are changes too, planned for Stamford Bridge, which will bring long-awaited benefits to the Club and you the fans.

Under Glenn Hoddle, we have a team we can be proud of. The Club is working hard to make The Bridge a stadium of which we can also be proud.

What goes on at Stamford Bridge on a match day and the parts played by the unsung heroes of the Club - its staff - are revealed in Blue is the Colour.

Our current squad are profiled and some of the famous fans who have always been attracted to Chelsea explain why they love the Club.

There is also a chapter on our sponsor Coors and the vital role they are playing in bringing great football back to Stamford Bridge.

Blue is the Colour is published at a very exciting time for Chelsea. It will not be long before once again we are seeing victory parades through our local streets and more silverware in the trophy cabinet.

With this book we can enjoy the triumphs of the past and look ahead to those of the future.

Ken Bates
Chairman

CHELSEA'S path to FA Cup victory in 1970 was a tough and turbulent one.

Looking back at pictures now it is easy to forget the blood, sweat and tears that marked the campaign.

# 1 How the Cup was Won

Chelsea's route to FA Cup glory.

The Club had enjoyed good cup runs before, and just three years earlier had reached Wembley in the 1967 final only to be defeated by Tottenham.

But there was something special about the FA Cup campaign of 1970 and as soon as the Club drew Birmingham in the third round there was a feeling that this year perhaps Chelsea's name would be on the trophy that had eluded them for so long.

That first match of the campaign set the pace for the rest of Chelsea's cup run.

The three goals that despatched Birmingham with ease at Stamford Bridge - one from Peter Osgood and two from Ian Hutchinson - served as an early warning to other clubs that Chelsea meant business.

Manager Dave Sexton had assembled probably the strongest squad in the Club's history made up of players who by the end of the season, would be heroes.

The goalkeeping skills of Peter Bonetti whose famous agility earned him the nickname 'The Cat', the solid defence of players like Ron 'Chopper' Harris, the midfield magic of Alan Hudson, the dazzling speed of winger Charlie Cooke and the deadly fire-

power of strikers Peter Osgood and Ian Hutchinson made Chelsea a force to be reckoned with.

But the Club's progress in the competition was nearly brought to an end in the fourth round against Burnley at Stamford Bridge.

Chelsea looked to be cruising to a 2-0 victory after goals from John Hollins and Peter Osgood. But the Lancashire side fought back, getting two goals and forcing a replay.

Chelsea fans who travelled to Turf Moor for the replay would have been forgiven for thinking the Club's luck had deserted them again in the FA Cup as in so many previous seasons.

Burnley went one up and held on to the lead until 18 minutes before the final whistle. It was Peter Houseman, the under-rated left winger, who put Chelsea back on the road to Wembley by unleashing a cracking shot from outside the penalty area into the Burnley goal.

Extra time - a taste of things to come for Chelsea - produced a goal from Tommy Baldwin and a second from Houseman to give Chelsea an entry into the next round and a trip south of the river to Selhurst Park.

But Crystal Palace were no match for a Chelsea side in full, glorious flow.

Osgood, John Dempsey, Houseman and Hutchinson all got

on the score sheet as Palace suffered a rout at Chelsea's hands. Palace pulled a goal back but the 4-1 score line shows how Dave Sexton's team now believed their name was already on that elusive cup.

The quarter-finals gave Chelsea even less distance to travel - their name coming out of the draw immediately after West London rivals Queens Park Rangers.

The match pitched Dave Sexton's now-rampant Chelsea side against one shaped by former Stamford Bridge favourite Terry Venables.

Venables had done much for Chelsea in the early to mid-1960s not only as a player but as a tactician and in many ways had sown the seeds of success that Sexton was now reaping.

It was ironic then, that Chelsea - and in particular Osgood - should use the muddy Loftus Road pitch to stage a show of strength and skill.

Osgood collected a hat-trick with David Webb also scoring as Chelsea dominated the game through their sheer class. Any neutrals watching that afternoon would have been in no doubt that they had witnessed potential cup winners in action.

Chelsea's name went into the draw for the semi-finals along with two of the country's top teams - Manchester United, Leeds - and Third Division Watford.

After a run of four tough cup games, Chelsea got the answer to their prayers at last and so lined up against Watford at White

Hart Lane for the semi-final.

Watford battled hard and cancelled out Webb's opening goal with an equaliser. But from then on it was Chelsea all the way - two goals from Houseman and a goal apiece for Osgood and Hutchinson ending Watford's dream, giving Chelsea the FA Cup's biggest semi-final victory for 31 years and putting the Club into the final for only the third time in its history.

Dave Sexton's team had an anxious wait to find out who

*The cup-winning squad of 1970.*
*Back Row, left-to-right, Ian Hutchinson,*
*Peter Osgood, David Webb,*
*Peter Bonetti, Eddie McCreadie,*
*Marvin Hinton, John Dempsey.*

*Front row, Tommy Baldwin,*
*Charlie Cooke, Ron Harris,*
*Peter Houseman, Alan Hudson,*
*John Hollins.*

*Captain Ron Harris introduces Princess Margaret to the team at Wembley*

*Right, Ron Harris and Leeds skipper Billy Bremner toss for kick-off.*

they would face at Wembley as Leeds and Manchester United slogged out two goalless draws before in their third meeting little Billy Bremner broke the deadlock and put Don Revie's Leeds into the final.

The scene was set for one of the greatest and most-thrilling cup finals of modern times.

But on Easter Monday 12 days before the final Chelsea suffered a major set back. Alan Hudson, the skilful 19-year-old midfielder and local lad who was already being talked about as the discovery of the season, tore his ankle ligaments in a game at West Bromwich Albion putting him out of both the final and replay.

Already widely regarded as the underdogs, Chelsea were forced to re-arrange the line-up for the final with Tommy Baldwin drafted into midfield to replace the injured Hudson.

On Saturday April 11th 1970 the Chelsea team of Bonetti, Webb, McCreadie, Hollins, Dempsey, Harris, Baldwin, Houseman, Osgood, Hutchinson and Cooke with sub. Marvin Hinton, ran out on to the famous turf of Wembley to face probably the biggest game of their lives.

Few neutral observers expected Chelsea to do more than put

on a skilful display before gracefully succumbing to Leeds' dominance.

After all, on paper Leeds certainly looked the better, more experienced side with players of international standing like Bremner, Jack Charlton, Gary Sprake, Norman Hunter, Johnny Giles, Eddie Gray and Peter Lorimer.

When Leeds took the lead in the 21st minute, there seemed little doubt of the result.

The goal, from a corner, was a typical thundering header from big Jack Charlton who was to pose a threat in the air to Bonetti and Chelsea's defence all afternoon.

Charlton's header which beat both McCreadie and Harris on the goal-line, summed up the differences between the teams, with Leeds always looking more dangerous in front of goal.

The skills of Gray dominated the left wing allowing him to feed a string of crosses into the Chelsea penalty area. The firepower of centre forward Mick Jones and Peter Lorimer were also constant threats.

But it was not all one-way traffic. Osgood put Chelsea fans' hearts into their mouths in the 38th minute when his shot beat Sprake only to be cleared off the line and scrambled clear by Charlton.

Three minutes later Sprake was beaten again - this time by a Houseman shot which rolled past the spread-eagled goalkeeper and into the Leeds net to level the score.

But with only a minute to half-time Leeds nearly went in front again as Gray unleashed a 20-yard shot which produced a diving save from the ever-agile Bonetti.

The second half, like the first, provided a wonderful spectacle of all that is best about British football with both sides determined to put on a show.

The hard-working Osgood, constantly looking for any opportunity to show off his skills, nearly put Chelsea ahead ten minutes into the half when he again beat Sprake but again his effort was cleared off the line, this time by an ice-cool Hunter.

A minute later at the other end Bonetti again saved Chelsea by blocking a point blank shot from Jones.

As the half wore on it looked increasingly likely that the first side to score would lift the trophy.

With less than ten minutes to go it seemed as if Gray would perform that task for Leeds when he shot from 22 yards out. Beating Bonetti, the shot looked as if it was the match winner, but thudded against the bar.

The Wembley crowd had just recovered from that near miss when, with the Chelsea goal again under attack, Jones shot from the edge of the penalty area, beyond the outstretched arm of Bonetti and into the Chelsea goal.

The Leeds fans were now certain the cup was theirs. But they had under-estimated Chelsea's spirit.

Just two minutes later and with four minutes to the end of full-time Chelsea won a corner. John Hollins stepped up to take it as

*Agony for Chelsea. Jack Charlton's header rolls between McCreadie and Harris for Leeds' opening goal.*

Chelsea fans hoped against hope that he could pull something out of the bag.

The ball flew into the area where Ian Hutchinson made contact, heading the ball past a stationary Sprake to level the scores once again.

The score remained 2-2 at full-time and the two teams squared up against each other again for 30 minutes of extra time.

But the hard-going of the pitch, which was in a terrible condition after a horse show a few days before, had sapped the players of energy and there never looked like being a deciding goal.

Of the near misses of extra time John Dempsey came closest first with a header that Sprake was forced to tip over his bar.

Leeds then had a couple of chances to decide the game - a Johnny Giles shot was cleared off the line by Webb after it had beaten Bonetti and an Allan Clarke shot ricocheted off the bar.

But at the end of 120 minutes the deadlock had not been broken - the first time an FA Cup had failed to be settled at Wembley and the first to go to a replay since 1912.

The two sides performed the traditional post-match lap of honour together but empty-handed, knowing that in 18 days they would face each other again, this time on the more hospitable surface of Old Trafford.

On April 29 the same Chelsea team emerged from the tunnel at Old Trafford although tactically Sexton had made some changes including switching the positions of Harris and Webb to enable Chopper to patrol the right flank and prevent Eddie Gray from causing the kind of damage he had done during the Wembley meeting.

But Leeds maintained their dominance early in the game and few were surprised when they took the lead when Jones latched onto a through ball from Allan Clarke and slotted it home, leaving Bonetti no chance.

The Chelsea keeper had only just recovered from a severe blow with Jones in the air which left him almost unable to walk. But his determination and professionalism meant he battled on.

*Shared honours at Wembley after 120 gruelling minutes, right; but 18 days later battle recommenced. Far right, Bonetti and Leeds Mick Jones in airborne action.*

Chelsea ended the half a goal down and once again it looked as if Leeds would lift the coveted trophy.

But, as at Wembley, Chelsea refused to doubt their own ability. The match began to turn and Chelsea began to dictate the pace of play with their patient passing game.

In fact, it was a superb passing movement between Hollins, Hutchinson, Osgood and Cooke that set up Chelsea's equaliser. Cooke chipped perfectly into the Leeds penalty area for a spectacular diving header from Osgood to level the scores for the third time and set up another 30 minutes of extra time.

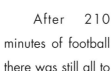

After 210 minutes of football there was still all to play for and with very little between the two sides, the 62,000-strong Old Trafford crowd realised the first goal would probably be the winner.

There were chances at both ends until just before the end of the first period Chelsea won a throw-in deep in the Leeds half.

Ian Hutchinson, possessor of probably the longest throw in football, launched one of his aerial assaults into the crowded Leeds goalmouth.

Jack Charlton rose above the white and blue shirts but could only flick the ball on and with immaculate timing and positioning David Webb saw his opportunity, leapt into the path of the ball and firmly headed into the Leeds net.

Hardly able to believe the match had turned their way at last, the Chelsea fans were over-joyed.

But it still was not all over. Sexton replaced goal hero Osgood with Marvin Hinton for the second period of extra time to strengthen the defence. It proved a wise precaution as Leeds threw everything at the Chelsea goal.

But it was to no avail. Referee Eric Jennings' whistle to end the longest final in FA Cup history was drowned out by cheers from the Chelsea fans - cheers repeated minutes later when Ron Harris raised aloft the FA Cup for the first time in the Club's history.

*Left, Osgood's stunning equaliser leaves Leeds' defenders rooted to the spot. Above, the party starts here! Below, "It's ours". Ron Harris displays the Cup at The Bridge.*

THERE can be few footballers who have in their time been an hotelier, undertaker, librarian and postman - all at the same time.

But former Chelsea goalkeeper Peter Bonetti found himself doing these and other tasks while running a guest house on the Isle of Mull.

Peter is now a freelance coach and loving every minute of it. He now lives in the Midlands with model/wife Kay and son, Scott, two, who seems to have inherited his father's football feet.

# 2 Where are they Now?

The heroes of 1970 – 25 years on.

# PETER BONETTI

Putney-born Peter joined Chelsea as an 18-year-old in 1959 and rapidly made a name for himself with his agility in the goal mouth - an agility that earned him the nickname 'The Cat'.

His career at the Bridge spanned two decades including Chelsea's League Cup victory of 1965 as well as the 1970 FA Cup - when he pulled off some remarkable saves to keep Chelsea's hopes alive - and European Cup Winners' Cup the following year.

When the highs of life under Dave Sexton were followed by the lows of relegation, Peter helped the Club regain its status in the premier flight, adding age and experience to the young side of the mid-seventies.

After more than 700 appearances for the Club as well as seven England caps, Peter left The Bridge in 1979 to move to the Isle of Mull with his family and four young children where he ran a guest house.

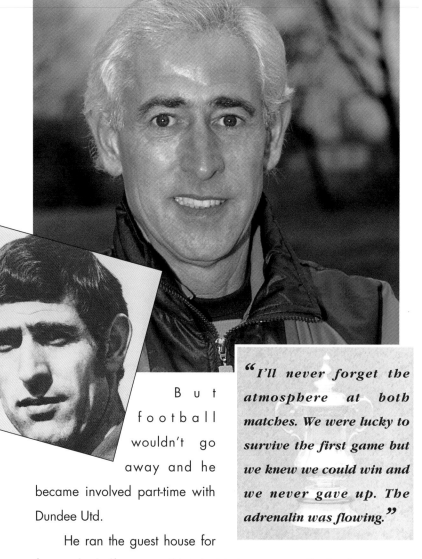

But football wouldn't go away and he became involved part-time with Dundee Utd.

He ran the guest house for four and a half years until he decided to return to England.

He coached the England under 21s from 1987-1990. Then the full squad 1990-1993 and now coaches under 21s.

*"I'll never forget the atmosphere at both matches. We were lucky to survive the first game but we knew we could win and we never gave up. The adrenalin was flowing."*

But David, now manager of Brentford, said: "I will always be grateful to Chelsea; that's why I went to QPR after Chelsea - because they seemed similar in outlook."

David, an East Ender, began his long career at Leyton Orient in 1964, playing under Dave Sexton briefly in 1965 before moving to Southampton.

He arrived at Stamford Bridge in 1968 and immediately became a favourite with the Chelsea faithful.

Although Dave Sexton first used him as a centre-half, David was used in a variety of positions during his time at Chelsea - from right back to central defender, as a striker and even in goal for one match when all three keepers were injured.

He left Chelsea in the wake of the departures of Osgood and Hudson. After three years at QPR he joined Leicester City for two seasons before moving on to Derby County and in 1979 joined Bournemouth as a player/coach, becoming manager a year later.

He became a player/manager for Fourth Division Torquay in 1984 before joining Southend as manager a year later. He was sacked in 1987 after differences with the Board but asked back the following year, leaving in 1992 after getting them into the Second Division.

Faced with relegation, Chelsea Chairman, Ken Bates asked David to be manager until the end of the 1993/94 season.

The Club finished mid-table and many fans were surprised when David's contract was not renewed.

*"There were crowds lining the street. I'll never forget handing the cup down to two Chelsea pensioners to hold for a moment. The look on their faces was magical."*

THE man whose goal won Chelsea the FA Cup in 1970 still has a soft spot for the Club - despite subsequent events at Stamford Bridge being unhappy for him.

For David rates his six seasons playing with the Blues as the happiest of his career. Few Chelsea players have such a packed CV as David - he played for eight clubs and is now managing his fifth.

# DAVID WEBB

THOUSANDS of young Americans owe their love of soccer to former Chelsea full-back Eddie McCreadie.

Eddie, capped 23 times for Scotland, is a director of the biggest youth soccer association in Tennessee with 130 teams, 40 coaches and 3000 pupils under his control.

It is a far cry from his days as a part-timer with Scottish club East Sterling.

He was brought south by Chelsea boss Tommy Docherty in 1962. Tommy saw potential in the 22-year-old Glasgow-born player and got him at the bargain price of £6,000.

Eddie was a mainstay for the Club throughout much of the sixties. But when his playing career ended his far-sightedness stood him in good stead for the job he is now performing.

Eddie and team-mate Terry Venables took coaching degrees in the early 1960s. The pair passed with distinction and both got their English Coaching certificates.

"Although it was hectic at Chelsea back then, the technical side of coaching interested me," said Eddie. "It was unusual at the time for Terry and I to do that. Most players only thought of doing it when their playing days were over. I'm glad I did it because coaching is now a large part of my life."

Eddie became Chelsea reserve team coach in the summer of 1974 when he realised his playing career was over. Within a few months he was manager and staring relegation to Division Two in the face.

# EDDIE McCREADIE

*"Just before Cup Final, I got bad stomach pains. I went to the doctor who diagnosed a hernia and said I must go in straight away. I refused. The operation was cancelled again because of the replay."*

Despite a lack of money to buy players, Eddie fashioned an exciting young team which took the division by storm playing attractive football.

But once back in the top flight Eddie expected more support from the board. When it failed to arrive he left the Club, crossing the Atlantic and taking over coaching at the Memphis Rogues who played in the National American Soccer League.

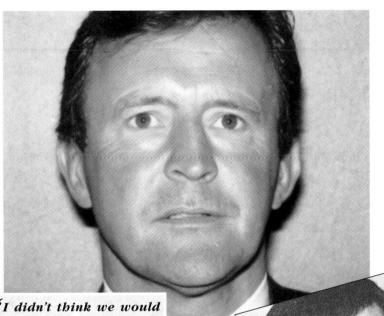

*"I didn't think we would win. The Horse of the Year show had made the pitch lousy but when we got the draw I knew we would win the replay if the fans were behind us.*

*At Old Trafford it was just a sea of blue and white."*

FEW players have worn a Chelsea shirt with such professionalism or commitment as John Hollins.

In his 591 games for the Club he gave his all and later as coach and then manager his commitment was never in question.

John, now coach at West London rivals Queens Park Rangers, joined Chelsea's youth scheme as a 15-year-old in 1961, signing as a professional on his 17th birthday.

He made an immediate impact and for the next 11 seasons commanded a regular first team place.

Although he played on occasions at right back, he was happiest in midfield and made the position his own in Dave Sexton's teams of the late sixties and early seventies.

So consistent was his game, he missed only four matches in five seasons and that was through injury.

But after Dave Sexton left Stamford Bridge, John became restless and after being dropped for several games, he joined QPR for £80,000.

"I was 28 and basically Chelsea thought I was too old," he said.

But John proved he had many more years as a player in him, moving to Arsenal in the 1979/80 season after four seasons at Loftus Road.

In 1983/4 John returned to Chelsea as player/coach. The Club was in the Second Division and dangerously close to the drop zone. John played 30 games and the Club won the Second Division title.

It was inevitable that John would become manager in succession to John Neal. But his near-three years in the hot seat were not happy ones as poor form on the field was followed by personal attacks on him from the Press.

Hardly surprisingly, John took a six-year break out of football and worked with commercial companies on sponsorship as well as being involved with several football consultancies.

# JOHN HOLLINS

ANYONE who thinks footballers are just selfish and money-grabbing would change their mind after meeting John Dempsey.

John's career in the game took him from Fulham to Philadelphia, via 200 games for Chelsea and FA Cup and European Cup Winners' Cup medals with the Club.

But now, in his words, the centre-half is giving something back working with people with learning difficulties.

He is a PE and sports instructor at Broadfields Social Education Centre in Edgware, Middlesex.

"It's a job I love and I wouldn't change places with anyone," said John.

He was signed by Chelsea for £70,000 from Fulham in January 1969 and soon built up a reputation for his solid defensive work.

He was capped 19 times by the Republic of Ireland and was set for a long career with Chelsea when a catalogue of injuries sidelined him for all but a few games in three seasons in the early seventies.

# JOHN DEMPSEY

John returned to the side in the mid-seventies but again injury robbed him of a regular place and in 1978 he went to America with Peter Osgood to join the Philadelphia Furies.

He was named Defender of the Year in a national competition staged by the American Press.

He returned in 1982 and became player/manager for Irish team Dundalk.

Three years later, John gave up playing and became full-time manager at non-league Maidenhead.

In 1986 he took a temporary job teaching at Barnet Council centres for the unemployed and the disabled. He enjoyed it so much, he stayed.

When the Centre needed a minibus, John wrote to Chelsea Director Matthew Harding hoping that he would donate £500 towards the target of £23,000. To John's surprise, Matthew paid for the bus.

*"I remember in extra time at Wembley when I nearly beat the Leeds keeper with a header but he just tipped it onto the bar. The noise of the crowd was tremendous."*

history is happiest now pulling pints behind the bar of Hunter's Moon, the hotel and holiday lodge complex he runs with his wife Lee in an idyllic setting near Warminster, Wiltshire.

With its view of the lake and the rolling countryside, it's a far cry from West London and Stamford Bridge, where he spent 17 years and chalked up a Club record of 783 games.

After leaving the Club Ron spent four seasons at Brentford as player-coach and then one season in management at Aldershot.

From there he bought a golf club near Swindon and built it up as a successful business.

"I had no experience in that type of business, but when you give up football, you've got to do something haven't you?" said Ron.

Ron sold the golf club and spent three years doing nothing but training his beloved greyhounds. "It was the break we needed and it recharged our batteries."

They then bought Hunter's Moon, a privately run 8-bedroomed hotel with eight lodges in the grounds.

"When I was a player, I spent a lot of my time in hotels and got to know good and bad ones. It's probably helped me in this business!" Ron said with a laugh.

Ron loves his life as a hotelier and is happiest behind the bar pulling pints for guests and customers.

"People ask me why I don't put shirts up and my medals but I won't. I don't want people to think I'm Jack the lad. If people want to see my medals and pictures, I'll show them but I won't push it. I'm proud of that time, don't get me wrong, but I won't bore people with it."

*"Walking up the tunnel at Wembley in 1970. It was magical! The longest walk in the world. But such a thrill. It is the dream of every footballer to play in the Cup Final at Wembley."*

RON Harris spent much of his playing career trying to shrug off the nickname 'Chopper' he acquired for his tough tackling.

But these days he is happy leading a quiet life in the West Country where he now runs a successful holiday village.

The only Chelsea skipper to lift the FA Cup in the Club's

**RON HARRIS**

VISITING American executives of US television company ABC may not know it, but the man who arranges their transport, accommodation and entertainment, used to entertain the crowds at Stamford Bridge himself.

Tommy Baldwin, a self-confessed golf fanatic, arranges golf trips for them at top courses as well as booking them into the top hotels and laying on executive transport.

It's a far cry from the shipyards of his hometown of Gateshead where he was working when he was discovered by Arsenal at the age of 15.

But after just 17 games in two seasons he moved across London to Stamford Bridge with George Graham going in the opposite direction.

He scored the first of his 92 goals for the Club on his debut but was never destined to be among the greats of The Bridge, and for much of his career with Chelsea was a reserve, although he is fondly remembered for his workmanlike approach to the game.

Tommy was drafted in by Dave Sexton for the FA Cup final of 1970 for the injured Alan Hudson in midfield and proved an effective replacement.

He stayed at Chelsea until 1975, spending some of the time on loan first at Millwall and then Manchester United.

He later became player/coach at Brentford where he found out life in the lower reaches of the professional game can be even tougher than at the top.

Although in his first season at the club it won promotion from the Fourth Division, there was no further progress for two seasons

and the entire team was sacked.

He then formed his own building company following in the tradition of his family.

A trip to America opened up links with ABC TV. Tommy is golfing mad and jointly started off corporate golfing weekends about five years ago with Peter Osgood.

# TOMMY BALDWIN

*" . . . Hitting the daylight as I came out of the tunnel and the roar of the crowd. It was so dark in the tunnel and the bright light as I stepped out and the big roar as I came out gave me a tingle down my spine and a shivery feeling that I will never forget."*

PETER Houseman spent ten seasons as a first team player at Chelsea, yet never attained the star status which some of his colleagues were awarded.

But he was a mainstay of the side, playing first in midfield then wide on the left with equal ability.

During the 1969/70 season he didn't miss a single game and put in some excellent performances during the FA Cup run, turning games in Chelsea's favour more than once.

He is, perhaps, best remembered for his outstanding performance in the semi-final against Watford at White Hart Lane, scoring twice in the 5-1 victory.

He worked hard during games, often dropping back to add support when needed. But he was also a beautiful crosser of the ball and often provided perfect crosses for frontmen Osgood and Huchinson to latch onto.

Yet he was always underestimated by Stamford Bridge crowds who liked their players to be a little more aggressive and colourful in character.

After being moved to left back at the beginning of the 1974/75 season, Peter joined the growing number of the 1970 Cup winning squad to turn their back on the Club, moving to Oxford at the end of the season.

His life was cut cruelly short when two years later at the age of 32, Peter and his wife Sally were tragically killed in a car crash.

# PETER HOUSEMAN
## (1945-1977)

ASK Chelsea fans to name their all-time eleven and the number nine shirt is likely to be filled by one man - Peter Osgood.

So when the Club needed a host to help out on match days at Stamford Bridge 'Ossie' was the obvious choice.

Relations between him and Chelsea Chairman Ken Bates had been strained for nearly ten years when they were brought together by fellow seventies legend David Webb.

That meeting led to Peter being offered the job as host in the sponsor's and executive areas on match days.

"I didn't need to think about it as I love the Club and was glad to be associated with it again," said Peter.

Peter made his debut for Chelsea in December 1964 at the age of 17 and scored twice - the first of his 150 goals for the Club.

A regular place in the main squad eluded him for several years and a broken leg sustained in October 1966 kept him out for the rest of that season.

But it was the classic Chelsea campaign of 1969/70 that brought out the real magic in Ossie's game. Now teamed up front with Ian Hutchinson, he became every defender's worst nightmare, poaching goals from nothing and making it all look so easy. He scored in every round of the FA Cup in 1970, including the remarkable diving header in the final replay.

It seemed only England manager Alf Ramsey was impervious to Ossie's ability and he was capped just four times. After a bust-up with Dave Sexton, Ossie left Stamford Bridge for Southampton in 1974, returning at the end of the seventies for

ten uneventful months before retiring. He then bought a pub in Windsor with Ian Hutchinson. The pair made it a flourishing business, selling it after five happy years.

He now runs Peter Osgood celebrity golf breaks and also has a Sunday football slot with Meridian TV and is a part owner of a restaurant.

# PETER OSGOOD

**9**

*"All the fans lined the streets to welcome us back and the Mayor and other dignitaries were there ... everyone had such a proud look on their faces."*

> **"I was hoping that we wouldn't have to go to a replay. I thought 'Wembley - what an awful pitch'. But then it was announced that it would be Old Trafford and I thought 'We always win there, it proved lucky for us'."**

IAN Hutchinson's playing career may have been untimely cut short through injury, but he managed to write his name into Chelsea's history with his uncompromising style.

His popularity on the terraces was never disputed - and has stood him in good stead in his career after football.

Hutch now has regular work on TV and cable TV football shows, while he is also chief steward at London's famous Alexandra Palace.

Although he was at Chelsea for six seasons after joining from Cambridge United for just £5,000 in 1968, he managed to play only one full season.

It was midway through the 1970/71 season that he sustained his first major knee injury that was to keep him out of the first team for nearly two years.

He made a full enough recovery to win his old place back - but was constantly troubled with knee problems until in February 1976 he was forced to quit the game for good at the age of 27.

He immediately threw himself into a new career as Chelsea's Commercial Manager.

The Club needed a frontman after being relegated to the Second Division and although Hutch had no commercial experience he took to the job easily and stayed there for two years.

"People who remembered me as a player put money into boxes, advertising and sponsorship," he said.

He then bought a pub at Windsor with Peter Osgood and used his experience of the catering and drinks business to act as a consultant to Brentford FC.

Eighteen months later, he became a publican again, this time in Taunton, Somerset until one Boxing Day flooding caused £70,000 worth of damage.

There followed a spell at London's famous Limelight Club for a year in the VIP lounge looking after the stars.

# IAN HUTCHINSON

A NEW generation of players are learning skills at the feet of one of Chelsea's most gifted players.

But the youngsters who are being coached by Charlie Cooke live thousands of miles from Stamford Bridge on the other side of the Atlantic.

Like his former team mate and one-time manager at Chelsea, Eddie McCreadie, Charlie has found the US has been the land of opportunity.

Charlie, capped 16 times for Scotland, is now a director of a soccer school in Cincinatti, Ohio, which he runs with former Wimbledon player Alfred Galustian.

Like many great players before and since, playing and coaching in America beckoned to Charlie when the English game had finished with him.

In Charlie's case, he went first to the Los Angeles Aztecs in 1978, then the Memphis Rogues and California Surf as a player before coaching the Wichita Wings.

But while many of his contemporaries returned to the UK to enter management or turn their back on the game, Charlie opened his own soccer school and has rode the crest of the wave created by last year's World Cup USA.

"America seemed a completely different world to me at first," said Charlie. "The stadia are so large and the attitude to sport is so different. I remember playing to crowds of 58,000 regularly."

Like Eddie McCreadie, Charlie signed for Chelsea after playing in his native Scotland. Although he broke the Club transfer record when signed from Dundee in April 1966 to replace Terry

## CHARLIE COOKE

**11**

Venables, he took a while to settle but once he had found his feet, his skills on the wing and in midfield became an integral part of the Chelsea Cup winning team.

*"It didn't really hit home what we had done until afterwards. I watched a film of it recently and we looked outclassed at Wembley. Leeds could have won by three or four or five even. At Old Trafford we were more confident."*

His contribution in both the final and replay should not be underestimated, especially his chip that set up Peter Osgood's diving header equaliser at Old Trafford.

> *"There have been millions of memories that I treasure, but the most vivid was the Stretford End at the Old Trafford replay. All the fans were waving their Chelsea scarves. All I could see was a sea of blue."*

MARVIN Hinton is probably best remembered by Chelsea fans for his calming influence as a substitute during the second half of extra time in the 1970 FA Cup replay.

But the episode was just one in a long career in football that took him from Charlton Athletic to Chelsea and at the end of his career to Barnet and later Horsham.

Marvin, who is now retired, is in no doubt which years were the happiest for him. He describes his 13 years with the Blues as the best time of his life.

"I spent a long time at Chelsea - I was even offered other Clubs while I was there. But I always said that I would stay with Chelsea until I was booted out," he said.

Marvin, originally from Croydon, used to play for Croydon Schools and joined Charlton at the age of 16 in 1956.

Then began, in John's words, the happiest time of his life. He was transferred to Chelsea for £35,000 - a large sum in those days.

"I wasn't surprised. Tommy Docherty had often asked me whether I would be interested in playing for Chelsea when I was in the England Under 23s (he won three under 23 caps). He kept dropping hints to me about it and then the official approach was made."

Marvin played 327 games during his career at The Bridge and so impressive was he in his early days at the Club that he was included in Alf Ramsey's 40-strong 1966 World Cup squad.

Despite being 36 when he left Chelsea, Marvin went on to play for Barnet, a non-league club at the time, although it had attracted outstanding players like Jimmy Greaves.

He then went on to Horsham where he spent two seasons before hanging up his boots.

# MARVIN HINTON

CHELSEA'S teams of the late sixties and early seventies were among the most exciting seen at Stamford Bridge - and much of that excitement was due to teenager Alan Hudson.

Born almost a stone's throw from the ground, Alan epitomised the swinging King's Road scene of the sixties that Chelsea's fame attracted.

But there was more to Alan than long hair and teenage good looks.

He made his debut in February 1969 at the age of 17 and within a year had become an integral part of Dave Sexton's team.

When Alan turned on the magic he could transform a mundane game into a classic. He could dominate a game and dictate its pace.

In many ways too much was expected of him at a young age and the one stage on which his skills would have shone - a Wembley FA Cup final - was denied him by a cruel twist of fate.

He collected an ankle injury in a game on the Easter Monday before the Cup Final against Leeds and was sidelined for the Wembley game.

Unfortunately, he was still not fit enough for the replay at Old Trafford and was forced to become a mere spectator when Ron Harris collected the Cup.

Over the next two seasons Alan conjured up some magical games but his form was inconsistent and after falling out with Dave Sexton, he was transferred to Stoke City for £240,000.

# ALAN HUDSON

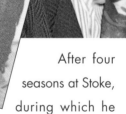

After four seasons at Stoke, during which he gained two England caps, he moved to Arsenal. He reappeared at Stamford Bridge in 1983 but was robbed of the chance to play for the Blues again through injury. He has since been a soccer coach, player in the US, nightclub owner and today is a sports columnist.

*"I was gutted at not being able to play in the final or the replay but I still feel part of the team that won. I remember the jubilant crowds and the celebrating. There was so much celebrating and so much pride."*

And as Chelsea's most successful manager to date, he reaped the rewards of his efforts. He cut his teeth as a coach at Chelsea under manager Tommy Docherty in the early sixties before moving across London to Leyton Orient as manager and then at Fulham and Arsenal as coach.

Once back at Stamford Bridge as manager he strengthened the squad with some astute signings, forming a side which could, on its day, out-play any in the land or even Europe with style and ability.

During his seven years' stewardship Chelsea won the FA Cup, European Cup Winners' Cup, reached the League Cup Final and ended every season in the top half of the table.

But stresses and strains began to show. There were disciplinary problems with players who had attained star status under him.

Acrimonious transfers followed and Chelsea's form suffered just as financial problems made winning more imperative.

Dave left Chelsea in October 1974, joining West London rivals Queens Park Rangers. In 1981 he moved to Coventry City, but left after two years when the then England manager Bobby Robson asked him to join the FA permanently as Official Technical Director of the National School in Lilleshall.

In 1990 Dave went to the Middle East coaching but his stay was cut short after six months when the Gulf War broke out. He returned to England and started scouting for various clubs.

*"When the whistle did go and we'd won, I couldn't believe it. Everyone went mad. I turned to go up the tunnel and Don Revie shook my hand. Frank Bough interviewed me but I was in a daze - quite choked."*

IN an era dominated by highly-vocal managers like Malcolm Allison and Brian Clough, Dave Sexton stood out like a sore thumb.

Quiet and modest, he put his energy and intellect into the game rather than headlines or interviews.

# DAVE SEXTON

**LORD RICHARD ATTENBOROUGH**

**Actor/Director**

# ③ The King's Road Club

*Famous fans share their love of the Blues*

"I'VE been a fan of Chelsea for 55 years. In 1941 I was at RADA and engaged to Sheila, the woman who is now my wife. Her father was a Chelsea fan. He loved all football but Chelsea and Fulham were his passion.

I started to go to matches with him. I even remember clearly where we used to stand.

We used to arrive at about 12 o'clock with masses of sandwiches and stand on the bank against those tubular things so Sheila wouldn't get pushed off. We went there for about five years until I went into the Air Force.

The first match I saw was in 1941. I was away in the Air Force for three years from 1943-1946. I couldn't get to any matches then, of course, but always kept track of the Club. When I came out of the Air Force, I was due to make the film *Brighton Rock*.

I needed to be as fit as I possibly could and so one of the producers of the film - John Boulting of the famous producing duo the Boulting brothers - arranged for me to get fit at Chelsea. He was also a devoted Chelsea supporter.

*Training for Brighton Rock. Richard Attenborough, centre, with left-to-right Tommy Lawton, Albert Tennant, Len Goulden, and Danny Winter.*

I was thrilled - training with players like Tommy Lawton, Len Goulden, Tommy Walker and Johnny Harris. I could scarcely believe it!

It was then that I became more than just a fan. I became really involved because I was accepted in the Club and I could go in and out as I chose and not just on a match day. It was a dream come true for me.

Every home game Tommy Lawton would leave two tickets for Sheila and I at the players' gate. I got to know Joe Mears (Chairman at the time) and he used to invite me into the Directors' Box.

I became Chelsea's Vice-President after the death of Lord Alexander. Joe asked me if I would like to take up the position. I was honoured to be asked.

Then I became a director and it got more hectic. I was all over the world for several months in the year and it became very hard to attend matches but I always kept track - no matter where I was -

*I only flew into London that morning and my plane was about three-quarters-of-an-hour late. My car met me at the airport got caught in the Wembley jam and we didn't move for what seemed like hours. I was frantic! I didn't know what to do. All sorts of thoughts ran through my head. Should I get out and run? I eventually got there 20 minutes before kick-off and, thankfully, I didn't miss the match. I missed the lunch. I'm glad, out of the two, it was the lunch I missed.*"

I would always phone to see how Chelsea were doing. I still do today. The girls at the desk always know it's me.

Then Joe died and Brian, his son, became Chairman. He asked me if I would join the Board. Oh, I can't describe the feeling. It was better than being asked to be Prime Minister!

I accepted with honour. I was a director for around five years, but it became more and more difficult to attend meetings because of my other film work.

In 1981, I was away for seven months filming Gandhi in India and offered Brian my resignation. He refused to accept it.

Then the East Stand came down and Ken Bates took over. We were all asked to resign and I gave my shares to the Club. Ken put quite a high price on them - several hundred thousand. In a match programme he kindly stated that he would build a stand for the disabled in return for me giving up my shares. That is something I really want to see happen.

After I gave my shares to the Board, Ken asked me to rejoin. I was deeply honoured but knew that I could not accept. My filming commitments were as hectic as ever and kept me very busy. He then made me life Vice-President. I was so thrilled.

I remember taking my son Michael at the age of nine to Chelsea for the first time. I will never forget how excited he was - with his scarf down to his feet and covered head to toe in badges and his rattle.

He is 45 now but I can still remember his excitement. He is still a Chelsea fan. Once a Chelsea fan, always a Chelsea fan!

I have four grandsons, and the two eldest, Sam and Tom, who are just the image of Michael when he was young and went to Chelsea - it brings it all back.

Their bedrooms are covered in pictures of Chelsea. They go to matches whenever I can take them, but I make it a condition that they play football in the morning before they come".

## TONY BANKS
### Labour MP Newham North-West

"I WENT to my first match at Chelsea around 1953. My first full season was 1954/55. That was particularly memorable because it was the only time we had won the championship.

I was lucky to have had that experience in my first full season and I never missed a home match that season either!

Like most people, it's where you first get taken. My Dad took me to Chelsea. I went with him and then, like most fans, I started going by myself when I was old enough.

We lived in Brixton at the time. By coincidence John Major (who is also a Chelsea fan) and I used to get exactly the same bus to matches. It used to go right over the river to the north side of Battersea Bridge. We used to get off and walk along by Lotts Road power station to Stamford Bridge.

Of course, we didn't know each other then - we were only lads. But the interesting thing is that we used to stand at different ends of the ground on match days.

The very, very best seats in the mid fifties were 12s/6d (62½p), the programme was 6d (2½p). It was a lovely programme and won prizes. I remember how I would tuck it down my front to make sure it didn't get damaged, because you wanted to get it home without a crease. I used to protect it with my life!

If the crowds were over 30,000 the programmes would sell out! I was disappointed often. It's funny, but the one I didn't get, I've managed to buy since.

It was Chelsea v WBA. I lost it and I went on a TV programme called The Exchange where you swap something for something you really want. I offered a personal trip round the Commons and afternoon tea on the terrace - I got ten offers! So the programme is safely in my collection 40 years later. Everything comes to he who waits!

I still have all my programmes from 1954/55 season and I avidly re-read them. I did collect a lot more from subsequent seasons but when I was at university, times were hard and I sold them all. I have never wavered in my support of Chelsea. Any real supporter knows the last thing you do is to change your football club.

It got more difficult to see Chelsea play when I was at university in York. Money was scarce and so I couldn't go very often but you can move away or abroad and your club stays with you.

I used to stand at the Railway end but I now enjoy sitting.

*"I couldn't afford to go to the Cup Final. I went to the semi-final but had to be content with seeing it on TV.*

*"I had only just left University and I couldn't afford it.*

*"My most vivid memory was Peter Osgood's goal. He was a wonderful player. I watch the video and it is still exciting today. We really were the underdogs then. But the pedigree of the Club was undeniable."*

I remember I used to be able to pick out the exact spot where I stood which was slightly to the right of the goal.

I could locate it by looking at the people. I never knew who they were but I could guide myself by looking for them.

You never knew their names - but you knew them and they knew you to nod to and they all had their own place on the terraces. I felt dead uncomfortable until I was in my regular spot and then I could concentrate. There was a familiarity about it.

If it was a particularly crowded match I would just push and wriggle through the crowd until I was in my place!

I try to go to every home match but politics sometimes gets in the way - but I get to as many as I can. I go with a friend of mine, whose partner hates football. My wife does as well so we go together".

### SEBASTIAN COE
### Olympic Gold Medalist and Conservative MP for Falmouth & Camborne

"I FIRST became a fan in 1967 at the age of 11. My Dad used to take me. My family were all Chelsea fans. We lived in Fulham at the time and it was just a short distance from the Club and so it became the most natural thing to do.

Chelsea was the first ground I ever went to - I even remember my first match. It was on New Year's Day in 1967 and Chelsea were playing Arsenal. I was sitting on the benches even then in the old stand which is still there. I can remember everything so clearly.

I had the scarf, posters - anything and everything to do with Chelsea. One of my most prized possessions is a letter I received at the age of 12 from Dave Sexton after I had written to him.

He was my hero at the time and I have a great admiration for him now and we are friends. He is one of the great coaches and thinkers of the game.

Up until the age of 20, I saw them play in their away kit most of the time because we moved out of London when I was quite young. I was about 19 when I realized they played in blue!

When I was a child, my Dad used to tie in visits to my grandparents who still lived in Fulham during the season so that was handy!

Then I started going fairly regularly. Because we lived in Stratford-Upon-Avon I used to go to most of the away matches.

I went regularly to see them play at Coventry, West Brom, Wolverhampton Wanderers and Aston Villa.

When I was at the University of Loughborough, I used to go down every other week on the train and stand in my usual spot at the Shed End.

I saw the Cup Final at Wembley. Beacuse our tickets came through Hillsborough, we sat in the Northern allocation, so there was I aged 14 in my Chelsea scarf surrounded by Leeds fans. It was a nightmare! Even the most devoted Chelsea fan had to accept that for a large part of that match, we were outplayed.

At the final whistle they just sat in silence, totally amazed at the end result. They had been ahead and the result had been a draw. Chelsea were like that. Never giving up 'till the end.

I remember leaving the ground absolutely elated and thinking we had lived to play another day.

I saw the replay on TV. It wasn't the same. Nothing compares to the atmosphere of being at a game.

I have both videos at home and it all comes back. I relive it a lot.

I stood up until a

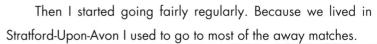

*" I saw the Cup Final at Wembley. Because our tickets came through Hillsborough, we sat in the Northern allocation, so there was I aged 14 in my Chelsea scarf surrounded by Leeds fans. "*

couple of seasons ago. Early on the Shed End was a good place for a student living on a student grant. But even when I was working I was happy standing in my spot in the Shed End on the left hand side.

I was a season ticket holder for ten years.

I moved back to London at the age of 23 when I got a job with the Sports Council.

When I became an athlete, it became more difficult because weekends took me out of London.

In fact when I was training for the Olympics in 1980, Paddy Pheiney from the BBC World Service, used to give me the latest results on air.

He used to say "To Sebastian Coe training in Rome, Chelsea won (or lost)."

My father has now moved back to Fulham and regularly goes to watch them. I try and watch them when I can but now I'm an MP, I'm in Cornwall at weekends and so life is a bit more complicated where Chelsea is concerned.

I was lucky when Chelsea had their good cup run. From the quarter final, Chelsea played on a Sunday, so I was able to leave my constituency on Saturday night and watch them play on Sunday. I was able to go to the Cup Final because of that and it was great!

I don't sit with Tony Banks but I have had a drink with him at half-time. We just talk football, not politics.

People recognise me but don't bother me, that's the good thing about Chelsea fans.

I live in Cornwall now and am president of a local supporters' branch with about 40 members."

### CLIVE MANTLE
**Actor**

CLIVE Mantle sends temperatures soaring as resident hearthrob Dr Mike Barratt in BBC TV's Casualty - the hit medical drama.

With his charming bedside manner it's hard to imagine him cheering Chelsea at The Bridge. But that's what he's been doing for over 30 years.

"I can remember exactly when my love affair with Chelsea began. It was in 1963 at the age of six, although I didn't go to see them play until six years later with my brother Richard after begging my parents to let him take me.

The first time I saw Chelsea play in the flesh was a 2-2 draw against Wolves.

It was pouring with rain and we were standing right by the dug-out. It was raining so hard that I was almost up to my ankles in water.

Wolves kept going ahead - I think they were 1-0 up or 2-0 up and then Chelsea pulled back. It was a magical moment. I was already hooked but nothing compares to the first time you watch your team play.

My brother could tell I enjoyed it and started taking me regularly. He is 13 years older than me and had a car so we could easily get to Stamford Bridge from our house in Barnet.

We went to away games as well. I can remember clearly

*Clive Mantle with Chelsea's medical advisor Dr Geoff Hughes.*

being the only Chelsea fan sitting in the posh stand at Carrow Road with my scarf round my neck. I was only young and my brother thought it might be safer if I sat.

Chelsea won 1-0 and I stood up and cheered and a middle-aged man threw a boiled sweet at me - it hit me smack on the forehead! That was my first inkling that there was a darker side to football.

We travelled all over the place to see them until I went to boarding school. Then it became difficult. I used to listen on the radio and get to a TV set if I could .

I used to get all the papers and cut out articles about Chelsea matches. I kept them all. I amassed seven or eight scrapbooks. I still have them.

When I was about 12, I broke my arm and while I was recovering at home, I drew a map called Chelsea Island. Everything was divided up like Cooke Bay etc.

I sent it to Chelsea and all the

*"I was in the St John's Parish Choir, Cambridge, at the time. We were at an official reception in France and I managed to watch the first half at the Lord Mayor's house on French television.*

*I saw the first goal when the ball trickled between Harris's and McCreadie's feet and then we had to go off and do this recital and so I thought Leeds had won.*

*I found out on the ferry on the way back that it had been a draw."*

players signed their part of the map and sent it back to me. I was so thrilled because there were drawing pin marks on each corner and so I KNEW they had put it up on the wall and signed it as they walked past. I was embarrassed because I had forgotten John Boyle - but he signed it in the middle of the sea!

After I left school at 18 and started at RADA I was able to go to every home match.

I stood in the Shed every game, on the right hand side. I always went there. I was superstitious about that. I felt if I didn't, they would lose.

Now I work on Casualty, it is very difficult to get to matches. We film ten months a year always at the weekend.

But the room where we relax always has Ceefax on and I can keep track of Chelsea. No-one dares change channels! I can't concentrate unless I know how Chelsea are doing.

Once when I was appearing in a Saturday matinee of Of Mice and Men the other actors kept me up to date with the latest Chelsea score every time they came on stage.

Now as soon as I get my filming schedules, I mark the matches I can get to in my diary.

I once went with Geoff (Hughes, Chelsea's medical advisor) to the executive box and to the dressing rooms and met the players. It was wonderful but I wouldn't like to go very often. It would destroy my dream.

As a supporter I have had my highs and lows with Chelsea, but as a supporter you have to have that. That's what it's all about.

I applied to become a member of Chelsea FC but they misread my signature. I did a swirly C on the form and they sent me back my card with the name Olive Mantle on it. I was mortified and couldn't show anyone else. I was so proud to be a member and wanted to show everyone and couldn't. So, somewhere in their records there is an Olive Mantle!"

## MATTHEW HARDING
### Director CFC

MATTHEW Harding comes from a family of Chelsea supporters. His earliest memory of the Club was when he first went to watch Chelsea play Newcastle in 1962 at the age of eight. He went with his Blues-mad dad Paul.

He even remembers clearly where he sat and how many times he went that season.

"The front row of the North Stand - and I went six times that season. It was a hell of a view - my chin was hanging right over the edge. After seeing that match, I was totally and utterly smitten and I have never wavered even with the terrible results we have had!" he added with a laugh.

Although born in Haywards Heath, Sussex, Matthew, like many of his friends looked to London for his football. For Matthew the only choice was Chelsea.

That season under manager Tommy Docherty Chelsea were promoted back into the top flight after just one term in Division Two.

"Tommy Docherty is someone I really admire for the way he started to shape the Club," said Matthew.

"He brought a sense of vibrancy and style to Chelsea.

I couldn't go to every match at that time but was always excited when I could. I didn't come from a monied family where my Dad could just say 'we'll go every week'.

I suppose that made me appreciate it all the more."

From then on, Matthew collected every programme and newspaper article that he could.

At the age of 11, he went to boarding school near Oxford and attending matches became difficult. He relied on his father to send him programmes and Club news.

"When I left school, I was able to watch Chelsea more regularly. Then I started playing first eleven County hockey. That was every Saturday for about ten years so couldn't attend matches but I still followed the Club avidly.

In 1982 I gave up hockey because I was getting on a bit and started to attend matches regularly again. By then I had four young children" (a daughter now 17, a son of 13 and 11-year-old twin boys).

"Once I had a family, I started taking them. I started to get season tickets because as well as my children, their friends started to come along.

I had eight season tickets in the East Stand Upper Tier. I still have those and also ten tickets in the North Stand".

In June 1993, he saw an article about the

> "I put £10 on at 10:1 for Chelsea to win the Cup. I carried the betting slip in my wallet at school and I remember Leeds were winning with 7-8 minutes to go and I tore it up neatly into four. Then Ian Hutchinson scored. I was over the moon. I still remember Sellotaping it up for the replay."

plans for Chelsea Village. He asked Janet Rainbow, who was running the Chelsea Pitch Owners' Appeal Fund, how Ken Bates was getting on with the development.

"I had never met Ken up till then. We had a meeting and it became very clear that a new stand had to be built that season. Planning permission was about to lapse and the Taylor Report said we couldn't have standing. We faced the prospect of having a two-sided ground which would have been ridiculous". Some £5m was needed to make the North Stand a reality and so Matthew provided the money.

"I admired what Ken was doing and it was clear that nothing was more important for the Club to spend its money on than the North Stand. I committed £5 million in the form of loan stock in Chelsea Village, which was non-interest bearing. As a result, the stand was completed within a year."

On 15 October 1993, Matthew was invited on to the Board. Until Christmas of that year, Matthew still went to matches in his jeans but changed into a suit when he got there.

"I didn't want my friends to think that I had deserted them," he said.

After the Cup Final, Glenn Hoddle signed Paul Furlong and Scott Minto with £2.5 million made available by Matthew who waived interest for the first six months.

Matthew, who made his money through his re-insurance business, also bought the freehold of the ground for £16.5m. He said "It is vital that Chelsea is allowed to play at Stamford Bridge. I'm a lifelong fan and I think I've demonstrated that."

## DAVID BADDIEL
### Comedian

DAVID Baddiel has been a Chelsea fan from the age of five.

"I feel a bit cheated really. My brother Ivor who is a couple of years older than me had been following them for two years before and I had really missed the momentum of the build up to the final.

I couldn't really understand the magic the Club had until then. I was too young, I suppose, but the magic of the replay did it for me. From then, I was hooked!

I had all the gear, the scarf, the strip and posters on my bedroom wall at my parent's house in Muswell Hill, North West London, and I've been hooked ever since.

Since then, I've never been able to support anyone else. That's Chelsea for you - my brother Ivor still supports and loyally watches them to this day.

I go to every home match even when I'm working. The schedule on Fantasy Football is very hectic but I never miss a game.

Once I even had a car waiting at the BBC to take me to the second half of the Real Zaragoza home game. I don't usually bother but it was 8.15pm and I was working late on Fantasy Football and I didn't want to miss the second half. I just got there with seconds to spare.

I'm always there in the West Stand cheering them on with Ivor. The fans recognise me and chat, but when the football starts, they leave me to it. That's the great thing about Chelsea fans - football comes first.

I forgot my season ticket once and had to blag my way in. My brother Ivor usually waits for me but didn't.

The football they play is great. I am a football purist, I suppose, and that means I don't go out desperately wanting Chelsea to win, but I love watching them play.

When I went to see them play Man Utd in the 1994 Cup Final I went with Frank (Skinner of Fantasy Football). They played really well the first half when the sun was shining. Second half it started to pour down and they lost. I drove home miserable and was being pestered by some Man Utd fans behind me. They were crowing '4-0 that's fantasy football'. I couldn't stand it so I turned off into a big housing estate and got lost for hours!

*"I became a fan when I saw them win the FA Cup replay in 1970 on TV. The match was very exciting to me at the time and I remember thinking what a magic club."*

So, it poured down, I got lost and Chelsea lost. I was inconsolable!

I had flown back from Newcastle specially for the match as well! Chelsea may have lost but they definitely weren't outplayed!"

Coors.

WHEN Ron Harris lifted the FA Cup at Old Trafford in 1970, there were many Chelsea fans who could hardly believe it.

For the history of The Blues is a turbulent one of near-misses, and missed opportunities.

Stamford Bridge has been home to some of the game's most-skilled players down the years and at times Chelsea sides have taken on - and beaten - the best not only in England but also in Europe.

But for a club that has spent most of its 90-year existence in football's top flight, Chelsea has precious little silverware to show for it.

# 4 The birth of the Blues

A brief history of Chelsea FC

From the outset Chelsea had its sights firmly set on becoming one of the country's top clubs.

There was no slow progression from works team or social club side through the minor leagues to the top.

Chelsea FC aimed straight for election to the Football League as soon as the club was formed in 1905 - and

got it at the first attempt without a player kicking a ball in a competitive match.

The club had been formed by wealthy business contractors Gus and Joseph Mears, owners of Stamford Bridge - at that time an athletic ground.

They dreamt of turning The Bridge into England's finest sports stadium - even rejecting a lucrative offer from the Great Western Railway which wanted to build a goods yard on the site.

The brothers used their wealth to assemble a team made up of some of the country's most skilled players of the period, including the 22st, 6ft 6ins goalkeeper Willie Foulke who had by then been capped by England.

*Far right. Early Chelsea programmes made up in humour what they lacked in information. Right. Sponsorship is nothing new! This advert is from a 1946 programme.*

The first home game - and Chelsea's third full fixture - attracted a crowd of 6,000 to Stamford Bridge. The 5-0 thrashing of Hull City showed Chelsea as one of the Second Division's class sides.

Word spread about Chelsea and the second home game - another win, this time 1-0 over West Bromwich Albion - brought 20,000 fans through the turnstiles.

By the end of the season more than a quarter of a million fans had watched Chelsea at The Bridge - including 67,000 for the Good Friday clash with division leaders Manchester United.

Chelsea gained promotion to the First Division the following season but, true to form, slipped back down again.

Another successful attempt was made in the 1911/12 season and by the time World War One broke out a clear pattern had emerged with Chelsea struggling to stay in the First Division but out-classing its rivals in the Second.

In fact, Chelsea ended the 1914/15 season in the relegation zone of the First Division. The League was suspended until September 1919, when the First Division was enlarged by two clubs - so earning Chelsea a reprieve.

The club enjoyed its first successful FA Cup run in 1915 when it reached the final but lost 3-0 against a vastly superior Sheffield United side at Old Trafford.

The immediate post-war period again saw fluctuations in fortune with the club gaining its first, if brief, spell at the top of the First Division early in the 1922/23 season but plunging back into the Second Division at the end of the following season.

Even though it took six seasons to get back into the top

flight, the fans stayed loyal with league gates at Stamford Bridge averaging almost 30,000 with 70,000 attending an FA Cup fifth round tie against Cardiff City.

The 1930s proved a fruitless decade for Chelsea in terms of trophies with hopes raised at the beginnings of several seasons after bright starts and often the arrival of big name signings only to fade as the campaigns wore on and the Club slipped down the table once more.

Despite this, crowds still flocked to Stamford Bridge. The Derby match against Arsenal in October 1935 attracted 82,905 and set a new attendance record at a league game.

During World War Two Chelsea played in

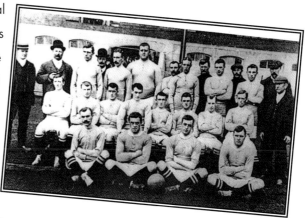
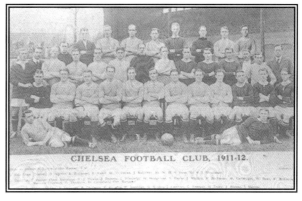

CHELSEA FOOTBALL CLUB, 1911-12.

*Chelsea squads down the years . . . top 1905, centre 1911-12, bottom 1912-13 . . .*

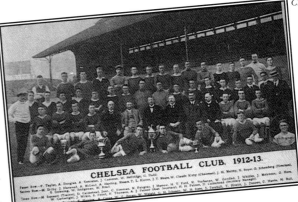

CHELSEA FOOTBALL CLUB, 1912-13.

the Football League South Group, one of the regional groupings which had replaced the national league as an emergency measure.

In 1944 Chelsea reached Wembley for the first time in its history in the final of the Football League South Cup losing to Charlton Athletic 3-1.

But the following year Chelsea were back at the famous stadium - and this time they beat Millwall 2-0.

Because many players were abroad on active service, teams were allowed 'guest' players from other clubs and the Chelsea side that day was boosted by two English internationals, Leslie Smith from Brentford and Len Goulden from West Ham.

Other famous names to appear in Chelsea blue during the War years in a similar way were Matt Busby, Walter Winterbottom and Scottish winger Billy Liddell.

Peace brought a flurry of signings at The Bridge, including Tommy Lawton, regarded as the best centre-forward of his day, from Everton for £11,500.

Peace also brought back the crowds to football and 53,000 saw Tommy Lawton's debut game - even though it was only a regional fixture before the resumption of the league proper.

*. . . top, 1920-21, centre 1921-22, bottom 1922-23 . . .*

*Ted Drake. He sought a New Chelsea*

An estimated 100,000 crammed into Stamford Bridge for the prestige match against Dinamo Moscow, the first of a four-game tour in November 1945 by the Russians. The score was 3-3.

Gates stayed high throughout the rest of the 1940s as Chelsea fielded exciting sides with a fair number of internationals. Yet although relegation was avoided, there was never a strong challenge for the Championship or the FA Cup.

The new decade seemed to bring a new determination, certainly in the FA Cup. Chelsea reached the semi-final against old rivals Arsenal and two early goals from Roy Bentley appeared to have booked the long-cherished Cup Final place.

But it was not to be. Arsenal fought back to force a replay, which they won 1-0.

Two years later history cruelly repeated itself when another semi-final against Arsenal ended all square but the North London side won an easy replay 3-0.

The two games were to be the high point of manager Billy Birrell's term at the club. But he left a lasting legacy in his youth scheme which not only brought much fresh talent into the side but made many clubs jealous.

His replacement, the pre-war England international Ted Drake, sought to create a 'New Chelsea' and on his appointment warned fans "Too many people come to Stamford Bridge to see a football match instead of cheering Chelsea. Let's have more people sleeping, eating, drinking Chelsea."

Drake's painstaking work paid off in Chelsea's golden jubilee season of 1954/55 when at last the Championship came to Stamford Bridge.

Although the season got off to a slow start for the Club, the results started to come their way and by Christmas they were second. By March 23, after an away win against Cardiff City they were top for only the third time in their history.

By Easter there was a four-point gap between leaders Chelsea and second place Wolves. Some 75,000 saw the game between the two at Stamford Bridge, with thousands more locked out after the turnstiles were closed at 2pm.

A Peter Sillett penalty in the 75th minute decided the game - and, effectively, the Championship.

But the momentum was not maintained - partly due to the ages of the Championship winning team, seven of whom were over 30.

During the next six seasons the highest placing was a lowly 11th. Even a chance to play in the European Cup as League Champions

*Peter Sillett.*
*He proved a Championship winner*

was rejected on the advice of the FA.

There was, however, a glimpse of things to come from the youth scheme. When the 1957/58 season kicked off a 17-year-old called Jimmy Greaves was given his first chance in the main squad. Ironically his League debut was against Spurs at White Hart Lane. He scored the equaliser that day and then three more in his next two home games.

During 1957's Christmas morning home match against Portsmouth he delivered a timely present for the faithful - four goals.

But Greaves' stay at Stamford Bridge lasted just four seasons - a total of 169 games during which he netted 132 goals. His stay may have been brief but it was eventful.

He scored five goals in a match on three occasions, became the first Chelsea player to score 100 League goals before his 21st birthday and during his last season set a club record of 41 goals in a season.

His final game before departing to AC

*... top 1925-26, centre 1933-34,*
*bottom 1930 ...*

... top 1947-48, centre 1949-50,
bottom 1955-56 ...

Milan, who had lured him with more money than the Chelsea board could afford, was a fitting tribute - a 4-3 victory over Nottingham Forest at The Bridge during which he scored all four goals.

During Jimmy Greaves' penultimate season another youngster from the youth scheme was thrust into the spotlight - a skinny, but agile, 18-year-old goalkeeper called Peter Bonetti.

With first and second keepers injured for a match against Manchester City in April 1960, the young Bonetti was given a chance - and performed with honours.

His quick reactions and agility earned him the nickname 'The Cat' - and an almost permanent first team place between the sticks for the next 19 years.

It was little surprise that Drake was ousted in September

Jimmy Greaves. 132 goals in
just four seasons for The Blues

Terry Venables. His tactical skills
helped with the rebirth of Chelsea

1961 after a poor start to the season - and no surprise that his replacement was his coach, former Scottish international Tommy Docherty.

Strict discipline became the Doc's orders and although it was too late to avoid relegation in 1962, the young side Docherty had assembled - its average age was 21 - were back in the First Division a year later and ready to take on the top clubs in the land.

By the 1964/65 season there was talk of Chelsea doing the Treble - League, FA Cup and League Cup. But the Championship slipped away from them in March and the FA Cup run ended in the semi-final against Liverpool. Only the League Cup was won in a two-leg final against Leicester City.

That opened the way for the Club to enter the Inter-Cities Fairs Cup for the first time. A good run lasted into the semi-finals against Barcelona when, after the score was all square over two legs, the Spanish side despatched Chelsea 5-0 in a third game.

Another good FA Cup run again ended with a semi-final defeat - this time 2-0 at the hands of underdogs Sheffield Wednesday.

Docherty's team, which had promised so much, was beginning to break up. The inspirational Terry Venables, whose tactical skills had played a key role in the re-birth of Chelsea, was sold to Spurs and George Graham departed for Arsenal.

Chelsea at last made it to the final of the FA Cup in 1967, only to see their hopes dashed by a 2-1 defeat at the hands of a Spurs side containing Greaves and Venables.

Relations between Docherty and the board, always fragile, broke down completely at the start of the 1967/68 season and former coach Dave Sexton was brought in.

Sexton was patient. With little in the way of spare money for new signings, he shaped a side that was two years later to win for the Club football's most-coveted piece of silverware - the FA Cup. (See Chapter One).

*Tommy Docherty, left, shares a joke with*
*Chelsea Director Richard Attenbrough during a break in training.*  45

Chelsea's defence of the Cup lasted only until the fourth round in 1971 when Manchester City roundly beat them 3-0 at The Bridge.

But the Club's sights were firmly on Europe and the Cup Winners' Cup, especially after the opposition in the two early rounds - Aris Thessalonikis and CFKA Sofia - were despatched easily.

It was against Club Bruges, in the next round that the hard work started. The first away leg saw the Belgians gain a 2-0 advantage.

The home leg, witnessed by a crowd of 45,000, saw Peter Houseman and Peter Osgood level the score at full-time. The finely-balanced match was put beyond Club Bruges in extra time - Tommy Baldwin and Osgood again ensured Chelsea a passage into the semi-final against Manchester City.

Chelsea won both legs 1-0 to return to Greece for the final against previous winners - holders Real Madrid. The fixture, played in front of 45,000 at the Karaiski Stadium, proved again that Chelsea could raise their game for the big occasion.

Peter Osgood put Chelsea ahead, only to see the lead snatched away by an equalising goal from Real Madrid to earn them a replay.

Real Madrid were widely tipped as favourites for the second match - but within 30 minutes Chelsea were 2-0 up. The Spaniards fought back and got a goal 15 minutes from the final whistle.

*. . . top year unknown, circa late fifties,*
*centre 1963-64,*
*bottom 1964-65. . .*

Despite attacking the Chelsea goal with venom in what must be the longest quarter-of-an-hour in the Club's history, Real failed to snatch an equaliser.

For the second year running Chelsea had landed a major trophy, this time against the cream of European soccer. The future looked bright. But it was not to be.

Despite a 21-0 aggregate scoreline in the first round defence of the Cup Winners' Cup against Luxembourg amateurs Jeunesse Hautcharage, Chelsea lost in the next round against Swedish side Atvidabergs.

The club was bundled out of the FA Cup by Orient and reached the final of the League Cup only to lose to underdogs Stoke 2-1.

The 1972/73 season ended with the club 12th in the First Division, their lowest level for ten years.

Worse was to follow the next season as relationships between Dave Sexton and some of his players deteriorated. Alan Hudson left for Stoke, Peter Osgood for Southampton and Dave Webb to QPR.

Few were surprised when that season Chelsea finished 17th and fewer were surprised when Sexton left the following October.

His replacement Ron Suart lasted less than a season and with three games left and the drop down to the Second Division almost inevitable, Eddie McCreadie was appointed manager. McCreadie saw the return of Chelsea to top flight football almost as a personal crusade.

Gates naturally plummeted with the drop of division and reached their lowest for 52 years.

McCreadie also had no money for new players. But he refused to be beaten. He shaped a young and ambitious team whose exciting football brought the crowds back and brought promotion within two seasons.

But just as it appeared McCreadie was to lead the club back to the glory days he saw as a player, he walked out, apparently angered by a lack of appreciation of his efforts at board level.

Ken Shellito was next on the managerial merry-go-round. He lasted just over a season to be replaced by former Spurs great Danny Blanchflower whose approach was spirited but his lack of managerial expertise could not stop Chelsea from

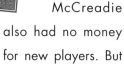

*Homecomings. Left, with the FA Cup in 1970, above with the European Cup Winners' Cup the following year.*

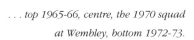

*. . . top 1965-66, centre, the 1970 squad at Wembley, bottom 1972-73.*

returning to the Second Division in 1978.

Another hero, this time the 1966 World Cup Final hat-trick scorer Geoff Hurst, took up the reins with Bobby Gould as his assistant. Again the future looked bright as the pair brought exciting football to Stamford Bridge again - but after an initial goal feast in true Chelsea fashion came a goal famine.

The Club sunk to its lowest league position ever, Hurst and

Gould departed in favour of John Neal - the Club's seventh manager in as many years.

Gates fell to their lowest-ever in Chelsea's

*Top. Bound for Greece and Glory. The squad of 1971 prepare for take-off for the European Cup Winners' ...p first leg. Above. Bring on Real Madrid. Celebrating the semi-final win against Manchester City.*

history and it seemed like the Club was drifting further away from the top flight rather than closer to it.

The1982/83 season saw Chelsea avoid relegation to the Third Division by a whisker. It was at this time that a former Chairman of Oldham Athletic, Ken Bates, bought the ailing Club with a mission to cut out the dead wood both on and off the field.

He described the club as a 'sleeping giant' - and was proved right.

Chelsea won the Second Division Championship in 1984 in style and John Neal was appointed a director, being replaced by John Hollins.

Hollins led Chelsea back to Wembley to win the Full Members' Cup 5-4 against Manchester City but his three-year period in the hot seat was dogged by patchy performances and poor results and was not a happy one.

Bobby Campbell, Hollins' replacement, could not halt the slide back into the Second Division but the Club stormed back the following year with a record 99 points from 29 wins.

Campbell, like Hollins, took his side to Wembley to win the Full Members' Cup - this time 1-0 over Middlesbrough. But once again Chelsea promised much but delivered little. The failure to fulfil the promise meant Campbell lasted three seasons before being replaced by Ian Porterfield.

*... top, 1977-78, centre 1980-81, bottom 1981-82.*

*. . . top 1983-84,
above 1985-6.*

Porterfield entered the transfer market with gusto and success in the newly-formed Premier League looked likely until a disastrous run of results plunged the Club back down the table.

Few were surprised when Porterfield was dismissed and it was to another former Stamford Bridge favourite David Webb that the Club turned to haul them back up the table.

But Webb's contract was only for three months and when the 1993/94 season kicked off it was with former England player Glenn Hoddle, one of the most-gifted of his generation, at the helm.

Hoddle had cut his teeth as a player-manager at Swindon, taking the club into the top flight for the first time in their history.

He began to shape Chelsea around his own fluent style of play and at first it appeared to be working but, as so often in the Club's history, things started to go wrong.

Although relegation was avoided, the Club's lowly position belied the attractive football.

Hoddle did, though, manage to get the club back into an FA Cup final for the first time in 24 years only to lose 4-0 to a rampant Manchester United side.

At least the club was back in Europe - this time in the European Cup Winners' Cup (see Chapter Six).

Chelsea finished a respectable but unspectacular 11th in the Premier League at the end of the 1994/95 season – a fact that made Glenn Hoddle's summer signings all the more remarkable.

Hoddle had always admired the talented Dutch player

*Mathew Harding, Chelsea Director*

DURING 1995 Chelsea achieved one long-held ambition which will have far-reaching effects on the future direction of the Club. Director Matthew Harding, who joined the board in 1993, bought the freehold of Stamford Bridge from landlords the Royal Bank of Scotland - and so ended the long-running wrangle over ownership of the ground.

Ever since Ken Bates took over as Chairman in 1982, his one ambition had been to buy the freehold of the ground.

Negotiations with the previous owners, a property development firm Cabra, became increasingly bitter and at one time it looked as if Chelsea would be playing their football at a neighbouring ground like Loftus Ro[ad]. But determination paid off. Although Royal Bank, which bought the groun[d] 1992, was more favourably dispo[sed] towards the Club than Cabra, the long-t[erm] aim was always for Chelsea to [own] Stamford Bridge and thereby have the r[ight] to play at their home in perpetuity.

The terms of the lease with the Royal B[ank] allowed the Club to buy the ground for £[?] million up to the end of the year 2012.

Matthew Harding, who made his pers[onal] fortune through reinsurance, had alre[ady] lent the Club money for players and to b[uild] the new North Stand.

Ruud Gullit, twice voted European Player of the Year. So when his Italian club Sampdoria gave him a free transfer, Hoddle pulled off what was at the time widely regarded as the shrewdest signing of a summer dominated by multi-million pound transfer deals.

At the same time Hoddle also signed Welsh international Mark Hughes, who was unsettled at Manchester United, to add firepower to Chelsea's strikeforce.

With such a strong squad and with Chelsea beginning to play the kind of attractive football Hoddle has so long dreamed of, the good times are set to roll again at The Bridge.

*The squad and management team of 1995/96.*

*..IN Hutchinson, Chelsea's Managing ..ector sees the 95/96 season as an ...ting time for the Blues both on and off ..pitch.*

*..the pitch, of course, we have had the ..val of Ruud Gullit and Mark Hughes ..h resulted in record season ticket sales ..record club membership.*

*.. the pitch itself has changed. It has .. extended from 110 yards by 70 yards .. 13 yards by 74 yards which should ..fit the way we play.*

*..more fans at Stamford Bridge will be ..to enjoy Channel Chelsea, our very own ..ouse TV station next summer when a ..huge screen will be suspended from* *the roof and planned as part of the North Stand wraparound. Away from the ground, we have just signed a new ten-year lease with the landlords on our training ground near Heathrow Airport and we will be spending a great deal of money on improving it.*

*We are also talking to the local council about running a community sports programme at Hurlingham Park. Hopefully that will be up and running in about two years so whether you want to play basketball or shove-ha'penny or cricket, you will be able to do it under the Chelsea umbrella".*

**Colin Hutchinson, Chelsea Managing Director**

# 5 Players in Profile

## DMITRI KHARINE

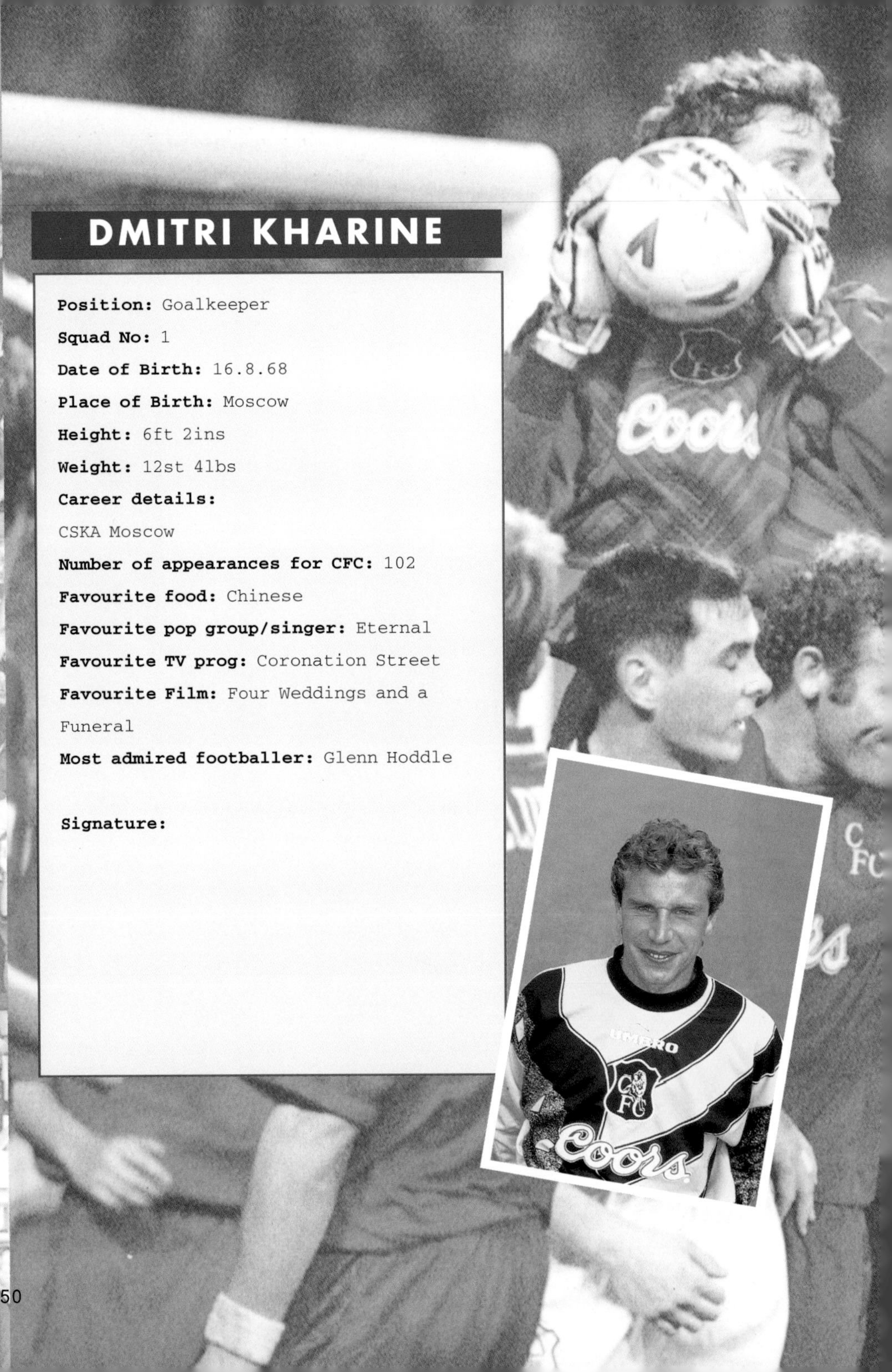

**Position:** Goalkeeper

**Squad No:** 1

**Date of Birth:** 16.8.68

**Place of Birth:** Moscow

**Height:** 6ft 2ins

**Weight:** 12st 4lbs

**Career details:**

CSKA Moscow

**Number of appearances for CFC:** 102

**Favourite food:** Chinese

**Favourite pop group/singer:** Eternal

**Favourite TV prog:** Coronation Street

**Favourite Film:** Four Weddings and a Funeral

**Most admired footballer:** Glenn Hoddle

**Signature:**

Information accurate at 11.9.1995

## STEVE CLARKE

**Position:** Defender

**Squad No:** 2

**Date of Birth:** 29.8.63

**Place of Birth:** Saltcoats

**Height:** 5ft 9ins

**Weight:** 11st 10lbs

**Career details:**

St Mirren

**Number of appearances for CFC:** 309.
Goals 9

**Favourite food:** Chicken and Rice

**Favourite pop group/singer:** Soul

**Favourite TV prog:** Channel 4 Racing

**Favourite Film:** True Grit

**Most admired footballer:** Nigel
Spackman

**Signature:**

## SCOTT MINTO

**Position:** Defender

**Squad No:** 3

**Date of Birth:** 6.8.71

**Place of Birth:** Heswall

**Height:** 5ft 9ins

**Weight:** 10st 7lbs

**Career details:**

Charlton Atheletic

**Number of appearances for CFC:** 29

**Favourite food:** Cooked Breakfast

**Favourite pop group/singer:** Eternal

**Favourite TV prog:** Only Fools and
Horses

**Favourite Film:** The Firm

**Most admired footballer:** Ryan Giggs

**Signature:**

## RUUD GULLIT

**Position:** Sweeper

**Squad No:** 4

**Date of Birth:** 1.9.62

**Place of Birth:** Amsterdam

**Height:** 6ft 3ins

**Weight:** 13st 12lbs

**Career details:**

Meerboys, Haarlem, Feyenoord, PSV Eindhoven, AC Milan, Sampdoria

**Number of appearances for CFC:** 5

**Favourite food:** Indonesian

**Favourite pop group/singer:** Soft Soul

**Favourite TV prog:** Nature Programmes

**Favourite Film:** None

**Most admired footballer:** Glenn Hoddle

**Signature:**

## ERLAND JOHNSON

**Position:** Defender

**Squad No:** 5

**Date of Birth:** 5.4.67

**Place of Birth:** Frederikstad (Norway)

**Height:** 6ft 1ins

**Weight:** 13st 5lbs

**Career details:**

Bayern Munich

**Number of appearances for CFC:** 138, 1 goal

**Favourite food:** Fish

**Favourite pop group/singer:** REM

**Favourite TV prog:** Only Fools and Horses

**Favourite Film:** JFK

**Most admired footballer:** Franz Beckenbauer

**Signature:**

## FRANK SINCLAIR

**Position:** Defender

**Squad No:** 6

**Date of Birth:** 3.12.71

**Place of Birth:** Lambeth

**Height:** 5ft 8ins

**Weight:** 11st 2lbs

**Career details:**

West Brom (on loan)

**Number of appearances for CFC:** 149, 8 goals

**Favourite food:** Chicken

**Favourite pop group/singer:** Backstreet

**Favourite TV prog:** Baywatch

**Favourite Film:** The Firm

**Most admired footballer:** Ian Wright

**Signature:**

## JOHN SPENCER

**Position:** Forward

**Squad No:** 7

**Date of Birth:** 11.9.70

**Place of Birth:** Glasgow

**Height:** 5ft 7ins

**Weight:** 9st 10lbs

**Career details:**

Rangers, Morton

**Number of appearances for CFC:** 67, 29 goals

**Favourite food:** Chicken and pasta

**Favourite pop group/singer:** Rap

**Favourite TV prog:** Match of the Day

**Favourite Film:** Schindler's List

**Most admired footballer:** Kenny Dalglish

**Signature:**

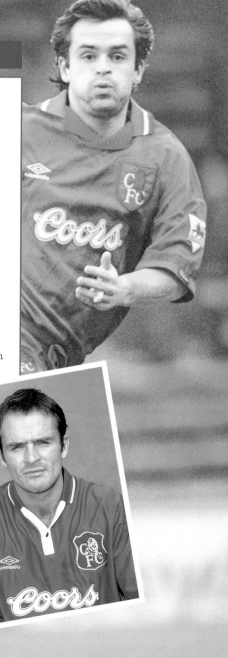

## MARK HUGHES

**Position:** Forward

**Squad No:** 8

**Date of Birth:** 1.11.63

**Place of Birth:** Wrexham

**Height:** 5ft 10ins

**Weight:** 13st 1lb

**Career details:**

Manchester United, Barcelona, Bayern Munich (on loan), Manchester United

**Number of appearances for CFC:** 5,1 goal

**Favourite food:** Pasta

**Favourite pop group/singer:** Diana Ross

**Favourite TV prog:** Coronation Street

**Favourite Film:** Letter to Brezhnev

**Most admired footballer:** Glenn Hoddle

**Signature:**

## MARK STEIN

**Position:** Forward

**Squad No:** 9

**Date of Birth:** 28.1.66

**Place of Birth:** South Africa

**Height:** 5ft 6ins

**Weight:** 10st

**Career details:**

Luton Town, Aldershot, QPR, Oxford Utd, Stoke City

**Number of appearances for CFC:** 53, 25 goals

**Favourite food:** Chicken and Pasta

**Favourite pop group/singer:** Aleia

**Favourite TV prog:** Coronation Street

**Favourite Film:** Good Fellas

**Most admired footballer:** Paul Furlong

**Signature:**

54

## GAVIN PEACOCK

**Position:** Midfield

**Squad No:** 10

**Date of Birth:** 18.8.67

**Place of Birth:** Eltham

**Height:** 5ft 8ins

**Weight:** 11st 5lbs

**Career details:**

QPR, Gillingham, Bournemouth, Newcastle

**Number of appearances for CFC:** 103, 20 goals

**Favourite food:** Italian

**Favourite pop group/singer:** Soul Music

**Favourite TV prog:** Roseanne

**Favourite Film:** A few Good Men

**Most admired footballer:** Glenn Hoddle

**Signature:**

## DENNIS WISE

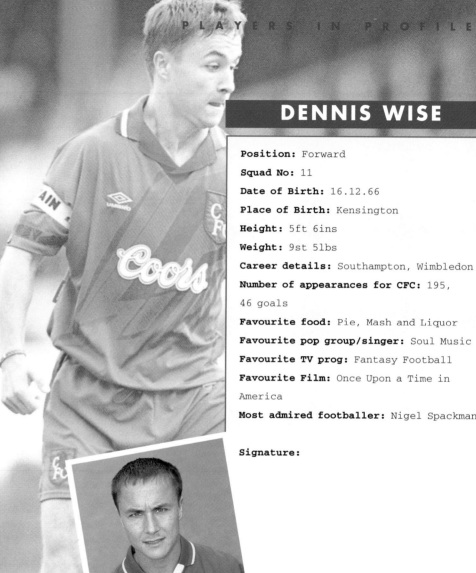

**Position:** Forward

**Squad No:** 11

**Date of Birth:** 16.12.66

**Place of Birth:** Kensington

**Height:** 5ft 6ins

**Weight:** 9st 5lbs

**Career details:** Southampton, Wimbledon

**Number of appearances for CFC:** 195, 46 goals

**Favourite food:** Pie, Mash and Liquor

**Favourite pop group/singer:** Soul Music

**Favourite TV prog:** Fantasy Football

**Favourite Film:** Once Upon a Time in America

**Most admired footballer:** Nigel Spackman

**Signature:**

## CRAIG BURLEY

**Position:** Midfield

**Squad No:** 12

**Date of Birth:** 24.9.71

**Place of Birth:** Irvine

**Height:** 6ft 1ins

**Weight:** 11st 7lbs

**Career details:**

No other clubs

**Number of appearances for CFC:** 55, 8 goals

**Favourite food:** Steak and Pasta

**Favourite pop group/singer:** Eternal

**Favourite TV prog:** Only Fools and Horses

**Favourite Film:** None

**Most admired footballer:** None

**Signature:**

## KEVIN HITCHCOCK

**Position:** Goalkeeper

**Squad No:** 13

**Date of Birth:** 5.10.62

**Place of Birth:** Cannington

**Height:** 6ft 1ins

**Weight:** 12st 2lbs

**Career details:**

Notts Forest, Mansfield Town, Northampton Town

**Number of appearances for CFC:** 94

**Favourite food:** Chicken

**Favourite pop group/singer:** Alexander O'Neal

**Favourite TV prog:** Match of the Day

**Favourite Film:** The Godfather

**Most admired footballer:** Glenn Hoddle

**Signature:**

## PAUL FURLONG

**Position:** Forward

**Squad No:** 14

**Date of Birth:** 1.10.68

**Place of Birth:** Wood Green

**Height:** 6ft

**Weight:** 11st 8lbs

**Career details:**

Coventry City, Watford

**Number of appearances for CFC:** 40,
13 goals

**Favourite food:** Chinese

**Favourite pop group/singer:**
Backstreet

**Favourite TV prog:** Match of the Day

**Favourite Film:** None

**Most admired footballer:** Mark
Hughes

**Signature:**

## ANDY MYERS

**Position:** Defender

**Squad No:** 15

**Date of Birth:** 3.11.73

**Place of Birth:** Hounslow

**Height:** 5ft 8ins

**Weight:** 9st 10lbs

**Career details:**

No other clubs

**Number of appearances for CFC:** 40,
1 goal

**Favourite food:** Chicken

**Favourite pop group/singer:** Backstreet

**Favourite TV prog:** Brookside

**Favourite Film:** The Fugitive

**Most admired footballer:** Glenn Hoddle

**Signature:**

## DAVID ROCASTLE

**Position:** Midfield

**Squad No:** 16

**Date of Birth:** 2.5.67

**Place of Birth:** Lewisham

**Height:** 5ft 9ins

**Weight:** 11st 1lb

**Career details:**

Arsenal, Leeds Utd, Manchester City

**Number of appearances for CFC:** 36,
2 goals

**Favourite food:** Aki Swordfish

**Favourite pop group/singer:** Backstreet

**Favourite TV prog:** Real McCoy

**Favourite Film:** None

**Most admired footballer:** Ian Wright

**Signature:**

## NIGEL SPACKMAN

**Position:** Midfield

**Squad No:** 17

**Date of Birth:** 2.12.60

**Place of Birth:** Romsey

**Height:** 6ft 1ins

**Weight:** 12st 4lbs

**Career details:**

Bournemouth, Liverpool, QPR, Rangers

**Number of appearances for CFC:** 242,
14 goals

**Favourite food:** Spaghetti

**Favourite pop group/singer:** None

**Favourite TV prog:** Only Fools and
Horses

**Favourite Film:** None

**Most admired footballer:** Kenny Dalglish

**Signature:**

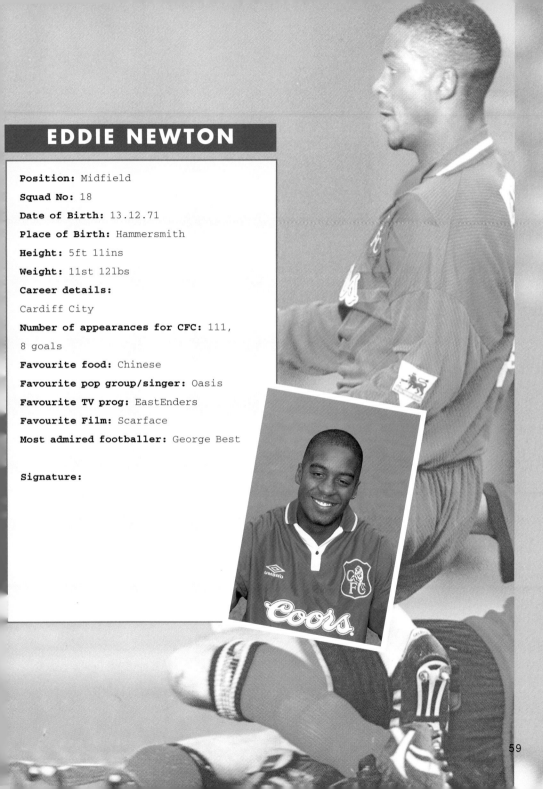

## EDDIE NEWTON

**Position:** Midfield

**Squad No:** 18

**Date of Birth:** 13.12.71

**Place of Birth:** Hammersmith

**Height:** 5ft 11ins

**Weight:** 11st 12lbs

**Career details:**

Cardiff City

**Number of appearances for CFC:** 111, 8 goals

**Favourite food:** Chinese

**Favourite pop group/singer:** Oasis

**Favourite TV prog:** EastEnders

**Favourite Film:** Scarface

**Most admired footballer:** George Best

**Signature:**

## JAKOB KJELDBJERG

**Position:** Defender

**Squad No:** 19

**Date of Birth:** 21.10.69

**Place of Birth:** Frederiks (Denmark)

**Height:** 6ft 3ins

**Weight:** 13st 8lbs

**Career details:**

Silkeborg

**Number of appearances for CFC:** 65, 2 goals

**Favourite food:** Bananas

**Favourite pop group/singer:** U2

**Favourite TV prog:** Men Behaving Badly

**Favourite Film:** A Few Good Men

**Most admired footballer:** Bryan Robson

**Signature:**

## GLENN HODDLE

**Date of Birth:** 27.10.57
**Place of Birth:** Hayes
**Previous Clubs:**
(As Manager): Swindon Town,
(As Player): Tottenham Hotspur, Monaco,
Swindon Town
**Honours:**
(As Manager): Swindon Town: Promotion
to Premier League 1992-93,
(As Player): UEFA Cup Winner; F.A. Cup
Winner,
(International): England: Youth, u21,
'B', 33 Full Caps

**Signature:**

CHELSEA fans have taken Glenn Hoddle to their hearts after just two seasons as player-manager.

In his first season with the Club he got it to the FA Cup Final for the first time in 24 years. The second season saw the Club reach the semi-finals of the European Cup Winners' Cup.

But what they don't know is that the former England and Spurs player was offered the manager's post at White Hart Lane at the same time as the Chelsea job.

Despite his association with Tottenham where he was a player for 13 years, he turned it down flat.

He has kept the story secret for more than two years but now he has won the respect of Chelsea fans he feels he can tell it.

"It wasn't an easy choice," said Glenn. "But I felt Chelsea was right - this was where I was meant to be. I can't say I wasn't tempted, because I was. It was a temptation for me to go back to my old club. I had supported them since I was 11!

If I had admitted this to the fans then, it would have been easier to win their trust much earlier, particularly with the rivalry between the two clubs.

But I was trying to defend a mate of mine who got the Tottenham job at the time and decided not to admit this publicly.

If I had admitted it, any suspicion by the Chelsea fans

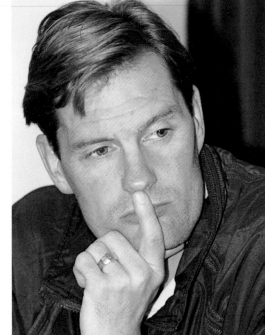

would have been killed off. But I feel the time is right to tell the fans now.

There was a suspicion when I first came to Chelsea by the fans and rightly so. But after the first season and the Cup Final, I feel that they are with me and I am happy about that.

Chelsea is the right Club for me. I knew that from the start."

Glenn had joined Chelsea as player/manager after combining the two roles to great effect at Swindon Town where he took the club into the Premiership for the first time in its history.

But at the end of the 1994/95 season Glenn announced that his playing days were over.

After 21 years as a player, most of them spent at the top of the profession, he decided to concentrate on management.

"I don't think being a manager only is ever going to be easy. It might be easier in the sense of the physical training.

But the mental side of management takes its toll and in that respect it will be easier just being a manager alone," said Glenn.

"Physically, I'm not as exhausted because I won't have to set time aside each day to train. I have a lot more energy to deal with management matters.

When I was abroad, I started to think about coaching and management. I succeeded in Swindon and I want to do the same at Chelsea.

I didn't decide suddenly to quit at the end of last season. It was something that was at the back of my mind that grew and grew. I'd been thinking about it for a few months before and my body was sending a few signals. I wasn't surprised at that stage - playing and managing takes its toll."

Glenn hadn't played a full game for about sixteen months before coming on as a sub in the home leg of the Cup Winners' Cup games against Real Zaragoza.

It was at that game that he decided to end his playing days.

"I just decided then that I would stop at the end of the season. I've finished playing earlier because I have been a manager/player - there's no doubt about that.

If I had been only a player, I know I could have carried on for a couple of seasons for sure, maybe until I was 40.

I'd had a terrific season and career and I felt it was right to go while I felt that everything was still intact. I wanted to go out on a good note, on a high."

That is exactly what happened. As Glenn left the Stamford Bridge pitch at the end of the game against Arsenal the crowd gave him an emotional standing ovation.

"I think I ended on a good note and got out relatively injury-free," he said.

"I'm a very lucky guy. I've had a wonderful career. I'm hoping that with a total manager's head on, I can continue my management career. I have only reached the tip of the iceberg as to how I want the game played.

At Chelsea, I've only played with my mind and now I want the team to play with my heart and my mind. I achieved that at Swindon and will achieve it at Chelsea.

I want to play the system I played at Swindon. It will be interesting to see what happens.

The sweeper system is the better system. Liverpool played it last season and they have been one of the best sides.

At Chelsea, I haven't been able to play totally how I want

*Hoddle leads the way in training. He plans to bring on Chelsea's young players.*

to. But I will. I will able have more energy to use now that I'm solely a manager."

Glenn intends to spend more time with the younger players, passing on some of his skills and preparing them for life in the first team.

As a player/manager he found he had to delegate certain aspects of the management side of the job to others. Now he plans to do more himself.

But he admits it will be a strain, sitting in the dugout without being able to go out and play.

"At a personal level, it will be a transition for me. It's going to be difficult not going out there and performing," he said.

"When the whistle blew at the Arsenal match and everybody started applauding, I thought, take this all in because it won't happen again," said Glenn.

"I'll always play football, of course, particularly in reserve games because I think there is a lot I can teach or get across to a player in a reserve game rather than in a first team game.

### Gullit on Hoddle

*"Glenn Hoddle was a major factor in my coming to Chelsea. There's no doubt in my mind about that. I've always had a lot of respect for him as a player and as a manager.*

*He tries to get teams to play passing football. That's the way I like to play.*

*He is also not the type of manager to shout and bawl to get his point over. He has his own special way. I like that. It makes such a change for me. Over the years I have had experience of different types of manager. It makes a welcome change.*

*Don't get me wrong. He isn't soft. When he's not happy, everyone knows about it."*

I think Graham (Rix - Youth Team Manager) and I have have an added string to our bow which not a lot of other clubs have.

Graham and myself don't just have the skills as players but we're just still young enough to play at reserve level which will bring kids on and inspire some of the pros that don't think they should be playing in the reserves.

I won't just play to play and take up a place that could stop a youngster's progression. But I think every now and again it's not a bad situation to have someone with vast experience play and make a team function well so that you can see whether these kids are going to be good enough for the first team."

Glenn's aim is to bring success to Chelsea by building up a skilled squad capable of playing in his style. That is why he spent most of the close season tracking and buying experienced players like Ruud Gullit and Mark Hughes.

Last season's European campaign also taught the relatively inexperienced squad some hard lessons which are standing them in good stead in the Premiership.

"The bottom line for supporters is that we need to bring success to Chelsea. It's been too long since we have seen a cup or some silverware," said Glenn.

He was pleased with the Club's progress in Europe last season, particularly as the squad was hit by more than its fair share of injuries.

"If someone had said to me you're going to get to a semi-final with 12 players out at different times,

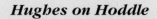

### Hughes on Hoddle

*"I played against Glenn many times when he was a player and, right from the start, I noticed his steely determination to win. That's never changed in all the time I have known him.*

*It hasn't changed now he is a manager and that's the secret of his success. His managerial skills are second-to-none. That's why I came to Chelsea and I've enjoyed my time here so far. It's not an easy ride, there's work to be done but with Glenn you know it will get done.*

*I knew he would bring the best out in me and he already has."*

*Top Left. Hoddle on the bench at Viktoria Zizkov. He wants Chelsea to be a major force in European football.*

*Hoddle at Stamford Bridge. He says Chelsea felt right to him from the start.*

I would have said 'I can't see how we are going to do that'.

People say no-one remembers a semi-final but we got there and I am proud that the boys did. You've got to remember that many of them had never played a European match before."

Glenn has a fixed idea of how he wants Chelsea to play.

I did that at Swindon and it worked. I have started it at Chelsea and so far it hasn't worked, but injury has hampered the development. I want certain players in key positions like they do in Europe but I firmly believe that you deal with whatever cards you get.

I am always striving for more. As a player, if I was told I had played well, I would try and do better next time and set myself even higher goals. As a manager, I have learnt you can't always be like that with players and have to find a balance. I'm learning that."

Glenn has been able to build up a management team to support him in these endeavours.

When I came to Chelsea I felt I wanted to put my stamp on things behind the scenes as well as the frontline.

I wanted people I knew and trusted around me and that's why I wanted Peter Shreeves and Graham Rix. They came straight away.

Peter has had every job in football! I first met him when he was my Youth Team Manager and he looks exactly the same as he did then!

### Wise on Hoddle

"The gaffer was always a player of quality with great skills. We always knew the time would come when he would hang up his boots and want to get on with being a manager.

He is a great manager just as he was always a great player. He has a very relaxed, easy manner with players and that brings out the best in them. He doesn't shout at us yet we know when he's not happy. I've got a lot of respect for the guy."

*Hoddle with Graham Rix, seated, and Peter Shreeves. He brought them in to strengthen Chelsea's management team.*

*The last game. Hoddle runs out of the Stamford Bridge tunnel for his final match as a player.*

He's been a youth team manager, a reserve team coach, a manager and in every aspect he's good.

He has probably seen me in more games than anyone. That really hit home to me when after my last match against Arsenal, he shook hands with me, turned and shook hands again and said 'thanks for the memories - there have been millions of them'! That really touched me and I knew he was well qualified to say it!"

Graham Rix, his number two, has proved a great ally to Glenn. "He is excellent with the kids and he enjoys his job. He has a lot of pride and to me that is important. He is really experienced and enthusiastic", said Glenn.

"At my last match, Gavin (Peacock) said something to me that I will never forget. One of their guys had an injury and we were playing some good stuff. We should have been three or four goals up within the first half an hour.

He suddenly turned to me and said 'Do you not fancy one more year, Guv?'. I had to laugh - it was quite funny. I had to think and then I said 'You just don't understand, Gavin, what it's like'.

In a way, it was a nice compliment. Players find it quite hard to understand the circumstances of being a manager one minute and the next we're out there on the pitch together.

## PETER SHREEVES

Peter Shreeves first met Glenn Hoddle at the age of 15 when he

was an apprentice at Tottenham. Peter was a coach there at the time.

"I have probabaly seen more of his matches than anyone! I remember when I first saw him play, how strong-minded and determined he was", said Peter.

"We always got on and were friends right from the start and it helps when we work together. He has so many ideas about management and he bounces them off me and I listen because Glenn's ideas are not off the wall but are always very focused. When he asked me to become assistant manager I didn't hesitate.

As I have been in management (he was manager at Tottenham and assistant manager QPR) I know the pressures Glenn is under and understand them and knew Chelsea would be a very exciting job and a challenging one.

I am proud to be Glenn's number two and know that under Glenn's guidance Chelsea will go far."

## GWYN WILLIAMS

Gwyn Williams has been with Chelsea since 1979 when he was appointed by Geoff Hurst as youth development officer. He then went on to become youth coach, first team coach and reserve coach before becoming chief scout four years ago.

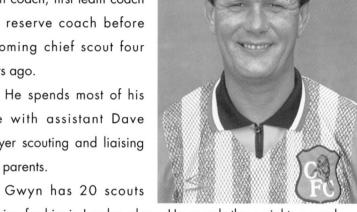

He spends most of his time with assistant Dave Collyer scouting and liaising with parents.

Gwyn has 20 scouts working for him in London alone. He spends three nights a week and weekends attending school games - looking for football talent.

*Chelsea in the Community was formed three years ago and ha*
*gone from strength to strength.*
*The roots laid down have developed into a very positiv*
*relationship between Chelsea and the Community. Former Fulha*
*professional Shaun Gore runs the scheme with the help of Assista*
*Football Youth Officer Michael Cole.*
*Shaun has a full licence to coach and runs soccer schools fo*
*youngsters in the half-term holidays. Up to a hundred young peop*
*can enrol for each course and they are always full.*
*A special match day package recently launched by the scheme wit*
*the chance to have a couple of hours coaching and a tour of th*
*Club including the dressing rooms, has been a huge success. Ther*
*is already a two-year waiting list.*

## EDDIE NIEDZWIECKI

Eddie took over as reserve team manager in 1991/92 season

after five years as Chelsea's goalkeeper. He was forced to retire in 1988 after an injury on his left knee.

He took over the youth team in 1988/89 for 18 months and then left for Reading to become assistant manager for 15 months. He returned to Stamford Bridge under Ian Porterfield.

"I enjoy the job immensely. It is important that the reserve team players are ready for playing with the main squad," he said.

*Pointing the way: Shaun Gore, left, and Michael Cole.*

## GRAHAM RIX

Graham Rix is the youth team manager and joined when Glenn became manager of Chelsea.

As well as a coach he describes his job as parent, social worker and pyschologist rolled into one, but wouldn't have it any other way.

He is responsible for the 15-18 year olds - a job he regards as a huge responsibility.

"How they are shaped at this stage influences their play and attitude to the game in the future," he said.

"They have got to be taught how to perform under pressure and with strength and finesse. I know how they feel. I've been there."

Graham was an apprentice at Arsenal and turned professional in 1975, making his professional debut in 1977.

In 1988, he went to France for four years and feels the experience taught him a lot.

"I learnt a lot about technical finesse from that time and I feel it helps me enormously in the job I do now."

In 1992 he went to Scotland to play for Dundee when he got the call from Glenn.

"Glenn is godparent to my children and we see each other as friends but he is very focused and knows what he wants from a team. I had no hesitation in accepting the job."

MANY Chelsea fans think the Club's rightful place is to be among the top European sides.

But the last time the Club played on the European stage Ted Heath was prime minister, decimalisation was about to come in and Slade were number one in the charts.

Twenty-three years is a long time to wait, but this season Chelsea took their place again among Europe's footballing elite.

Defeat in the 1994 FA Cup final allowed the Club to go through to the European Cup Winners' Cup because the victors Manchester United were already committed to taking part in the European Champions, League.

Chelsea prepared for their European campaign with a series of pre-season friendlies against European teams - and the players soon came to realise that playing in the Premiership is no preparation for Europe.

The English Premier League may be the toughest in the world - but taking on the cream of European football with all their skills was another matter.

The Club played in a three-way tournament in Denmark with Copenhagen and FC Koln from Germany.

# ⑥ Back in Europe

Highlights of the 1994/95
European Cup Winners' Cup matches

*Paul Furlong in action against Athletico Madrid in the pre-season Makita Tournament.*

Assistant manager Peter Shreeves recalled: "Although we won our match against Copenhagen the players found the opposition's movement off the ball very hard to cope with.

Basically there was a lot more of it than we were used to in the English game and after we played Koln and were well beaten by them, we knew we had to get our thinking caps back on."

The pre-season Makita Tournament with Arsenal, Athletico Madrid and Napoli gave the Club more experience of the style of football they would be encountering in Europe.

So when the draw for the first round pitched Chelsea against the Czech side FK Viktoria Zizkov, with the first leg at home, the squad was well-prepared for the change of style.

And the start could not have been better. The clock seemed to have turned back 23 years as Chelsea took the upper hand in the opening game against Viktoria Zizkov with The Bridge buzzing with excitement.

Two goals in four minutes - one each from Paul Furlong and Frank Sinclair - seemed certain to have sealed the Czech side's fate. But Zizkov hit back, squaring the score with two goals by half-time.

Chelsea were learning the lessons of European football the hard way and with the away goals rule a constant danger, it was vital they won this match.

David Rocastle and captain Dennis Wise made sure they did - Rocastle with a 35 yard shot and Wise with one of about 30 yards to give Chelsea a useful two-goal advantage to take to the Czech Republic.

The away leg proved to be a less dramatic affair apart from an amazing penalty save from Dmitri Kharine to keep the match goalless. In fact the keeper had already pulled off a number of fine saves to deprive Zizkov of a home win but when Anthony Barness tripped Zizkov forward Karel Poborsky in

the area, it seemed like the Czech team would get the result they wanted.

Petr Vrabec hit his penalty to Kharine's left only to see the keeper block it and then turn aside the follow-up shot from Jiri Casko.

The 0-0 scoreline was enough to keep Chelsea in the competition and a second round tie against Austrian league champions Austria Memphis.

Again the first leg was at The Bridge only this time the opposition were experienced European campaigners - and the tight man-marking proved it.

Glenn Hoddle's choice of players, already badly affected by injuries, suffered another set back when Frank Sinclair was stretchered off after just 15 minutes with a torn ligament.

With the Austrians closing down Chelsea players all over the pitch, the result always looked like a goalless draw with Chelsea's only real chance coming in the 80th minute when Rocastle thundered a shot under Austria Memphis keeper Wohlfahrt only to see it bounce off his shins and hit a post.

After the match Glenn Hoddle was full of praise for his side, saying he was disappointed with the result but not the performance. He felt certain Austria Memphis would open up

*Above. A David Rocastle long range shot against Viktoria Zizkov produces Chelsea's third goal.*

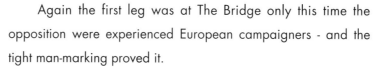

*Left. Paul Furlong celebrates scoring against Viktoria Zizkov.*

69

*Right. David Rocastle shoots at the Austria Memphis goal. The effort was deflected. Below, Glenn Hoddle celebrates victory over the Austrians.*

more on their home ground - and that would be just the opportunity Chelsea needed to score a goal.

He was proved right - and what a classic goal it turned out to be.

Five minutes before half-time a Memphis shot was parried by Erland Johnson with the ball falling to Spencer inside his own half but clear of the Austrian defence who had come forward.

Spencer ran 70 yards before lobbing the ball over the despondent Wohlfahrt and into the net.

In the second half Andy Myers, making his European debut on his 21st birthday, had a goal disallowed for off-side and while Narbekovas equalised for Memphis with 17 minutes of the tie remaining, Chelsea defended strongly. And with away goals counting double the Club went through to the quarter finals.

Glenn Hoddle said the Austria Memphis away game was the best performance by a Chelsea side under his stewardship and few would disagree.

The Club had to wait until February for the first leg of the quarter finals - away to the Belgian side Club Bruges, who co-incidently had been one of Chelsea's victims in the Club's victorious 1970/71 Cup Winners' Cup campaign.

But torrential rain and storms had turned the pitch at the Olympiastadion into a bog in parts - hardly a stage for the best of Europe's players to display their skills.

Bruges looked the better side, particularly down the right where Sven Verheyen was causing trouble and most of Chelsea's chances came from set pieces.

The scores stayed level until the 83rd minute when the Belgians whipped in a free kick from the edge of the area, which came off Verheyen and into the net as Kevin Hitchcock, making his European debut, was sent the wrong way.

The Chelsea keeper made no mistake with a spectacular diving save from a Lorenzo Staelens overhead kick in the dying seconds of the game - a save that kept Chelsea's hopes alive for the second leg.

*Scott Minto in action against Club Bruges.*

After playing almost totally in defence during the first leg, a change of tactics from Chelsea for the home leg saw the players take the game to Club Bruges.

The switch of styles paid off. With the 28,661 crowd full of optimism and in fine voice, Chelsea went ahead after 16 minutes through Mark Stein, who got his knee to a Craig Burley header across the Belgians' goalmouth.

Just over 20 minutes later Paul Furlong put the game beyond Club Bruges with a sidefooted shot from a Stein cross - the end result of a fine passing movement Furlong himself had

*Gavin Peacock holds off a challenge from Real Zaragoza's Santiago Aragon.*

started off on the edge of his own six yard box.

Although Club Bruges battled to get a goal back, they found no way through the Chelsea defence and so Chelsea's name went into the draw for the semi-finals with Arsenal, Sampdoria and Real Zaragoza.

But there was to be no London derby, or a chance for Chelsea to take on the Italian cup winners. Instead the draw landed the Club with the Spanish side - a club that enjoyed a reputation for creative football of their own.

Chelsea learnt this the hard way in the first leg away.

Within 25 minutes of the start Zaragoza were two up - even though the Spaniards were having trouble with the Chelsea defence's offside trap.

Zaragoza were happy to sit back and defend their two goal advantage - but Chelsea still found they were dangerous on the break and Zaragoza's third goal came when Frank Sinclair was dispossessed in the centre circle and within a couple of rapid passes Hitchcock was picking the ball out of the net for the third time that evening.

Zaragoza had given Chelsea a mountain to climb in the home leg - but Glenn Hoddle was certain his team were going to go all out.

With a highly-charged crowd, at times it looked like the miracle was about to happen as Chelsea drove forward.

Paul Furlong grabbed Chelsea's opening goal with an astonishing piece of good luck when keeper Juanmi hammered a pass back straight onto Furlong's arm and into the goal.

But luck was not to be on Chelsea's side.

Another brilliant passing move by Zaragoza, deftly finished by Santiago Aragon, levelled the scores.

Chelsea once more had it all do. But with the crowd behind them, the players knuckled down and tried.

Frank Sinclair volleyed home a Furlong header to make it 2-1 and with four minutes to go Furlong again supplied the header which Mark Stein got a knee to and sent it into the Zaragoza net.

Chelsea had staged a remarkable comeback after the disappointment of the first leg - but found the going just too tough against the side that won the final a month later against Arsenal.

After the game Glenn Hoddle said, had the chances gone

*Paul Furlong is eager to get on with the game after scoring against Real Zaragoza.*

in, then they could have scored the five goals needed after Zaragoza got the away goal.

He also praised his players for their determination - and then announced he was to quit as a player.

Chelsea's first European campaign for 23 years had ended at the semi-final stage after a gutsy series of games of which everyone at the Club can be proud.

And if Glenn Hoddle has his way, the Club will be back in Europe next season.

# 7 Count-down to Kick-Off

Behind the scenes at Stamford Bridge on a match day

WHEN the referee blows his whistle at 3pm to start the game all eyes are on the pitch.

But long before the teams and fans arrive, Stamford Bridge is a hive of activity.

A match day starts at 7am, eight hours before kick-off, when head groundsman John Anstiss arrives. John is responsible for the care of the playing surface as well as all the repairs and maintenance of the ground.

John has been working for the Club since 1968 and became head groundsman in 1985.

He is the second generation of his family to be a groundsman. His father George was head groundsman from 1968-1985 and John's first job at the Club was working under him.

"We were a team then and we are a team now. My Dad always insisted on that. Teamwork builds success and I try to do that now," he said.

Half an hour later the fresh food starts arriving ready for Chelsea Catering to start preparing the meals.

By 8am the first

chefs have arrived and are beginning to work on some of the 250 lunches they will serve in the restaurant on match day.

A lot of preparation has already been done a couple of days before match day, including ordering hamburgers and meat but to ensure the catering side of the Club maintains its excellent reputation, as much as possible is done on the day itself.

By kick-off a small army of staff are working away behind the scenes, including a total of 130 waitresses, kiosk operators, kitchen porters as well as ten supervisors and three managers.

Keeping an eye on all this are Chelsea Village Catering director Peter Price and operations manager Claudio Fontana.

Keith Lacey, Chelsea's safety officer, arrives at Stamford Bridge at 7.30am for a briefing meeting with chief steward Ian Jenkins. Keith oversees security and safety on a match day.

Before each game a number of safety and security checks

*Top right. Taste test. Claudio Fontana, Chelsea Village Catering's operations manager checks the food. Right. The best bar none. Chelsea Village Catering director Peter Price.*

## ON A MATCH DAY

800 portion of chips

650 sausages

1200 burgers

10 boxes of crisps

400 pies

240 chicken steaks

Coors
Extra Gold

40-70 kegs of
Coors consumed

401 cokes

401 orange juice

## ARE SOLD

**Figures for North Stand sales**

are carried out - all designed to minimise disruption to supporters but to maximise their safety and security.

Tasks such as checking the 36 emergency telephones, firefighting equipment and fire extinguishers and security cameras and ensuring they are in good working order are carried out.

There are around 15 security cameras inside and outside the ground. These are important for crowd counting and monitoring.

Only when Keith is satisfied there are no problems can supporters be let into the ground.

The stewards are briefed in more detail at around 9am by Keith and Ian. There are around 500 stewards in all including agency stewards. Most have jobs during the week but work as stewards on a match day out of love for the Club.

*Channel Chelsea presenter Graham Dene interviews Mark Hughes.*

Gary Staker is one such example. During the week, he works for the BBC. On a match day he is the senior steward in charge of the players tunnel - a job he has done for the past 12 years. He looks after the home and away players and keeps any uninvited vistors away from the tunnel area.

"That's a full time job in itself!" he said with a laugh.

At 8am Ron Knowles the electrician arrives. Ron checks that all the lights are in perfect working order.

Ron is part of John Anstiss's team which also includes Lee Chubb assistant groundsman, Barry Brown, Lee Deegan and Trevor Pitworth. Between them they have 60 years experience.

On a match day the grass is cut with two gigantic mowers - a 42-inch Allett, which John calls the Rolls-Royce of mowers, and a 36-inch Ransom. The pitch markings are marked out and the goal nets are put up.

Pitch preparation is really a week-long business and much of match day will be spent on general maintenance and cleaning up around the stadium from repairing a seat in the stand to unblocking a sink.

*Above. A cut above the rest. John Anstiss and his team. Top right. Doug Johnson, Stadium Manager.*

The team are allocated areas around the ground on a match day and are in constant touch with each other and Keith Lacey by radio control so that they can be on the scene in minutes.

John, unlike some groundsmen, is not precious about the

pitch and all his team know how to care for it.

"I'm happy to pass on what my Dad taught me so that our pitch is always a cut above the rest," he said.

Stadium manager Doug Johnson arrives around 8.30am. Although Doug is responsible for the whole ground on non-match days, he is back-up for Keith on a match day.

"If Keith needs me for anything, I'm there," said Doug who was a policeman for over 30 years and as a Chief Superintendent at Fulham Police station was responsible for policing football matches.

At 9am Stamford Bridge reception opens and the phones start ringing almost immediately. The Blues reception desk is a hive of activity on a match day.

Reception team Teresa Conneally and Fiona Barker deal with the non-stop flurry of activity.

Teresa, who has worked for Chelsea for 19 years, is press secretary and prepares the press list on a match day, issues the passes and sorts out the programmes for players, apprentices, executive members and the press.

"I love Chelsea and can't see myself leaving here - they'd have to carry me out in a box!" she said.

Teresa also organises the family day for the Club each year as well as various other social events for the players such as testimonial dinners.

Fiona organises staff meals on a match day, books tickets for disabled supporters as well as answering hundreds of phone calls.

Chelsea Sportsland also opens at 9am, although the staff have been in since 8.15am finishing the restocking so that there is plenty of everything for the fans - from the latest strip to souvenirs.

General manager Tony Marks, who is also buyer, designer and window dresser, and his staff of 11 - four full-time and seven part-time - make sure the Chelsea fan doesn't want for anything.

*Bottom left. Service with a smile. Teresa Conneally, left, and Fiona Barker. Left. Counter culture. Tony Marks in Chelsea Sportsland.*

It really gets busy around 11am with hardly any room to move until kick-off at 3pm.

**TOP FIVE THINGS SOLD AT CHELSEA SPORTSLAND**

1. Strip.
2. Baseball cap.
3. Sweatshirts.
4. Scarves.
5. T-shirts.

As well as British fans, Chelsea has a large European following with Norwegians, Belgians and Germans. Most diehard European fans buy from the catalogue mail-order service.

The shop stays open during the match and closes at 4.45pm. Nearly 100,000 people a season come in and shop on a match day.

Also open at 9am is the box office. Tickets start selling immediately - not only for that day but for future dates.

Like Chelsea Sportsland, the office has been busy before it

*Coors*

opens to the public, in fact, Box Office manager Eddie Barnett and his team have often been processing tickets the night before a match day.

Every ticket still unsold has to be printed the night before to be sold on a match day. Sometimes the team are there until midnight.

*Right. Just the ticket.*
*Eddie Barnett serves at*
*the box office.*
*Far Right. Kitman*
*Terry Byrne.*

Eddie has three box offices selling tickets under his control in the East, North and West stands.

Eddie, originally from Hartlepool, joined Chelsea in 1990 and first introduced the computerized lottery to Chelsea. He became box office manager a year ago.

Eddie fell in love with Chelsea the minute he walked through the gates. But he has never seen a game because he is always too busy.

"I don't mind. I love my job and the Club - that's why!" he said.

Eddie's team consists of: Hazel Farrant and Marianne Smith, reservations are dealt with by Richard Fleming and Anita Blowden. The box office is also a family affair - Eddie's wife Pat also works there.

Kit manager Terry Byrne also arrives at around 9am. As well as looking after the kits on a match day, Terry is masseur and assistant physio.

He joined Chelsea originally as a part-time masseur on match days. When the kit manager's job came up, he became a full-time member of staff.

"I'm a lifelong fan. Working for Chelsea is a dream come true," said Terry, who is known as Terry the Taxi.

Until last season Terry also washed all the kits. "Before I came to Chelsea I didn't even know how to operate a washing machine. I soon learned fast," he joked.

He washed all the kits - from main squad to the youth and reserve teams.

He learnt the tricks of the trade when it came to shifting stubborn stains and mud - not to mention occasional blood.

Terry has to wait to get the team sheet before laying out the kits but at 10am he lays out injury kits, prepares match balls, referees kits, as well as players' drinks.

He also checks that players' boots have been cleaned properly by the apprentices and the correct types of studs inserted.

Terry knows that many players have a favourite type of shirt. "Dennis Wise prefers short sleeved shirts while Craig Burley only likes long sleeved ones," he said.

At 10am physio Mike Banks arrives. Mike joined Chelsea last season from

**SOAP POWDER**

SOAP POWDER

**TERRY'S TIP FOR A MUD FREE WASH**

*Presoak dirty and stained kits in Vanish, scrub in hot water and then wash. It never fails!*

Tottenham where he was assistant physio.

He prepares equipment and emergency first aid and strappings for players who need them. He also checks each player thoroughly before the match warm up for muscle tears.

Mike also checks that his field kit is stocked with everything he needs - from swabs to stop bleeding to sutures for dressing wounds as well as dozens of other items from aspirins to splints.

The Club also has a medical team consisting of Dr Hugh Millington, a consultant at Charing Cross Hospital, and Dr Geoff Hughes, a consultant in accident and emergency at the Bristol Royal Infirmary who is also medical adviser to the BBC show Casualty.

They are there on a match day in case of severe injury to the players or the fans.

At 10.30am Breda Lee arrives and starts to prepare the players' lounge ready for the players' wives and children. The players' lounge was the idea of Glenn Hoddle when he joined Chelsea as player/manager.

Previously there was nowhere for the players' wives and children to sit and have a drink before and after a match.

Breda has been a Chelsea fan and volunteer since she saw them play Arsenal on Christmas Day 1942.

"I was living in North London and came with a friend on the spur of the moment. I liked the match, loved Chelsea and the love affair began. I wanted to help the Club in any way I could," she said.

There followed spells in the ticket office, general office and now she is the players' tea lady and also looks after the match mascots.

Although she now lives in Poole, Dorset, she never misses a home match and hasn't missed an away match in more than 30 years.

She also wears Chelsea blue for every home match when she can.

The mascots arrive with their parents at 1pm and are welcomed by Breda and mascot co-ordinator Kim Eatwell.

Kim who works in the commercial department has a year-long waiting list for mascots.

"It's lovely to see their faces as they run out on to the pitch," says Breda who has two grandchildren of her own. All her family are Chelsea mad.

Kim organises the mascot applications that come in during

*Below. On the bench. Physio Mike Banks.*

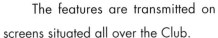

the week.

"I couldn't miss seeing them on a match day with their Chelsea football strip on!" said Kim.

Kim and Breda escort the mascots around the dressing rooms before the game. They watch the match from the Directors' Box.

At 11am the production crew for Channel Chelsea arrive. Channel Chelsea is the Club's own TV station and was set up at the end of 1994 when the new North Stand was completed.

Channel Chelsea opens from 12.15 on a match day right through till around 6.30pm with match highlights, interviews with everyone from directors, players and fans, and nostalgia spots.

The features are transmitted on screens situated all over the Club.

This season, Virgin Radio DJ Graham Dene is the host.

The team consisting of cameraman Richard Warwick, technicians Jim Postins and Steve Roberts, executive producer David Utall and Gina Repton (schedules) set up their equipment and look through their schedules for

*Top right. Kim Eatwell. Right. Their big day. Chelsea Mascots before kick-off.*

interviews. They liaise closely with co-ordinator Michelle Dyson from the Club's marketing department.

At noon Neil Barnett, who runs Clubcall and edits the match day programme and the Chelsea newspaper Onside, arrives at Stamford Bridge.

Neil makes the on-pitch announcements and pre-match and half-time presentations.

These vary from the man-of-the-match to Chelsea Pitch Owner share certificates which are handed over to the new shareholder by the player of their choice.

Jane Wilkins and Judy Walker, Glenn Hoddle's secretaries, have been in since 9am. They help out on switchboard as well as prepare the boardroom guest list and type up the list of player changes.

"We both love the job and match day

is the most important part of it. We wouldn't miss it for anything," said Jane.

Judy and Jane have a working relationship that is rare to football - they job-share.

"We are both able to work part-time in a job we love and spend the other half of the week with our children," said Judy.

She joined Chelsea nine years ago. Her father used to take her to matches as a child. It was her love of the Club that prompted her to write asking for a secretarial job.

After having her daughter Jessica she got part-time work in a hospital but it wasn't the same. Jane and Judy kept in touch and when Jane got pregnant and said she wanted to go part-time the answer was obvious - to job-share. Jane has been with Chelsea for ten years.

The first guests of the Club arrive at noon and are greeted by Carole Phair, the Club's commercial manager.

She has been at the stadium since 9am when she prepared the stewards' brief which gives details of any special guests, including match and ball sponsors. She also checks the hospitality areas and liaises with caterers.

Carole's first contact with Chelsea was a few years ago – she was then working for a travel company and arranged a promotional trip to La Manga in Spain for the team.

She joined as sales and marketing executive in 1993, becoming commercial manager two years ago. Carole's job is wide and varied and she loves it. "No two days are the same and that's why I love it!" she said.

During the week she sells corporate hospitality facilities, programme advertising and seasonal boxes as well as match day hospitality.

On a match day Carole and her team - Kim Eatwell and Michelle Dyson, sales and marketing executive - take care of various guests such as executive members and box guests.

At 1pm Carole arranges the presentation of the match ball to the sponsors and co-ordinates the match day tours with former Chelsea greats Peter Osgood, Alan Hudson and Paul Elliott who are now hosts.

Paul is match day host for guests of sponsors Coors while Ossie performs the task for Chelsea.

*Taking care of guests.*
*Left, Commercial manager*
*Carole Phair and, above,*
*Judy Walker, left, and Jane Wilkins.*

*Above. Safety first. Keith Lacey briefs stewards. Top right. Read all about it. Programme sellers do brisk business. Right. Doing the bizz. Mick Amer and his famous Cabin.*

Around 150 people are taken on a tour behind the scenes each match day.

At 12.30 the stewards - Chelsea stewards and agency stewards - are issued with their yellow jackets, or orange ones for fire marshalls.

They are then briefed by Ian Jenkins and match commander Supt David Fitzsimmons.

Ian has been a steward at Chelsea for 30 years and chief steward for 15 when his father Sid retired.

One of the best-known faces around Stamford Bridge, Mick Amer, gets in around noon and sets up Mick's Cabin.

During the week, Mick manages the post room - franking up to 3,500 letters a day as well as programme subscriptions - a job he has done for over 11 years.

But for 25 years Mick, whose nickname is 'Bizz' because he is always so busy, has sold old programmes and posters on match days.

He has been involved with Chelsea for more than 40 years

and has done all sorts of jobs for the Club - from cleaning, general maintenance and even operating the turnstiles in the fifties.

He is a familiar sight to Chelsea diehards and is an ardent fan himself. If there's a programme a collector needs, Mick's the man they see.

The match day programme sellers start doing brisk business at around noon when fans start arriving although some have been at the stadium since 9am setting up and unloading programmes.

Bridge Builder Promotion agents start to arrive at this time to sell lottery tickets on a match day. The lottery, which raises money for the Club, is held every week and there are cash prizes to be won. Season ticket holders are

automatically entered.

Other items for sale range from autographed drawings of the players to miniature models of Chelsea buses.

The Chelsea Pitch Owners' (CPO) office across the road from Stamford Bridge also sells merchandising and shares to raise money to buy the freehold of Stamford Bridge.

*Promotion chasers: left to right, Joanne Doyle, Pippa Robinson and Janet Rainbow.*

The promotions team is made up of special projects manager Janet Rainbow, Pippa Robinson, who is in charge of the lottery, membership secretary Joanne Doyle and Nicola Porter, membership assistant.

At around 2.30pm, the ballboys arrive. Their job is to collect and return any stray ball that goes off the pitch. They are situated at various points on different sides of the pitch.

At 15 minutes-to-three the ballboys, who are selected from neighbouring schools, line up at the tunnel ready for the teams to come out.

Then at 3pm the referee blows his whistle, the countdown is over for another game and the match begins.

---

*Stamford Bridge lost two unsung heroes in 1995 when George Anstiss, former head groundsman and Sid Jenkins, former chief steward, died.*

*Until six months before he died, George (pictured below with Eddie Barnett) had lovingly gone to the Stamford*

*Bridge every Friday night and marked out the pitch lines for the match the following day.*

*"The Club and the pitch were his life. He lived and breathed Chelsea and was a familiar figure at the Bridge for 50 years.*

*Everyone knew and loved him," said close friend Eddie Barnett.*

*George originally was a starter at the dogtrack but became Chelsea's groundsman when the Greyhound Racing Association closed in 1968.*

*"I loved the job from the start. I loved nurturing and*

*looking after the pitch. It was like another child to me that needed looking after," George said just before he died.*

*George retired in 1985 and his son John took over. John had worked alongside his father since 1968 and he had taught him everything he knew.*

*George's wife Flo even worked in the old Club shop for a while on match days.*

*Sid Jenkins (pictured right, with son Ian) became a steward at The Bridge when he returned from the War after serving in the Royal Artillery. He did virtually every job from selling tickets to marshalling crowds and conducting VIP tours.*

*He also became the first supporters' club secretary after retiring from his job at the Inland Revenue.*

CHELSEA and Coors have become a winning team since they linked up through their sponsorship package.

Coors Extra Gold, the award-winning American premium lager, was best known in the UK through its TV adverts featuring John Ratzenberger, the postman Cliff from Cheers, until it signed up with Chelsea.

# 8 Coors & Chelsea – A Winning Team

The story of a successful sponsorship

southern Club.

The company put a large amount of money behind Coors, and after the success of McEwan's with Blackburn and Newcastle, it was hardly surprising that football sponsorship was discussed as one of the ways to raise its profile.

Robin Alexander, at the time Chairman and Managing Director of

The lager is brewed and marketed in the UK by Scottish & Newcastle plc which has become one of the biggest sponsors in football with deals backing Blackburn Rovers, Newcastle and Glasgow Rangers.

But because the South of England has the largest proportion of lager drinkers, the company decided on a tie-up with a go ahead

William Younger, S&N's Southern trading arm, was able use his valuable experience of working in other areas of S&N where they had secured football sponsorship.

"We wanted to link Coors, a quality product, with a quality team - a mover and shaker in the football world," said Robin.

"We had looked all over the South of England but London was the obvious choice as our market research had shown that there are a greater proportion of premium lager drinkers there than anywhere."

Attention focused on Chelsea. It was no secret that the club's previous sponsor was not going to renew its deal at the end of the 93/94 season.

Strengthening the links. Chelsea Chairm[an] Ken Bates and directors Yvonne Todd a[nd] Colin Hutchinson during a tour of Willi[am] Younger's Nottingham Brewe[ry]

Chelsea seemed to fit the bill and when William Younger researched the club their findings delighted them on all counts.

Chelsea was in the key area for premium lager drinkers and the Club's pedigree was a good match for Coors. William Younger saw a bright future for the Club - a belief that was strengthened when Chelsea signed up Glenn Hoddle, as manager in the summer of 1993.

By Christmas 1993 the deal was in the bag but had to be kept secret until the previous sponsorship deal expired.

"They played exciting football and their image was a classy, quality one. I knew they were destined for greater things and they have proved me right." said Robin.

"Here is a Club that is now enjoying huge success and will continue to do so. It attracts huge media attention because of the exciting football the team plays."

The Coors-Chelsea link was kept under wraps to gain maximum publicity at the beginning of the 1994/95 season.

But by that time Club and sponsor were already working closely together.

The company entertains important clients at Stamford Bridge on match days - last season alone more than 1,000 guests enjoyed Coors' hospitality - and employs former Chelsea player Paul Elliott to greet and mingle with guests.

"Paul is popular and has a great rapport with everyone," said Robin.

Michael Jarvis, Coors Brand Manager is in no doubt about the benefits to both Coors and Chelsea that the link-up has brought.

"We feed off each other," he said. "Coors has obviously benefited by being associated with a dynamic, exciting Club of worldwide renown.

Football is part of the fabric of society and that's where

Coors wants to be.

We have gained extensive TV and press coverage not only in London but nationally. Chelsea's location was also important to us because South East England represents more than half of the UK's premium lager market so it is the area with the greatest opportunity for Coors."

Michael believes sponsorship can be more effective than advertising.

"It has a remarkable power in making the brand part of people's lives.

The success of Chelsea on the pitch has obviously given the Coors brand exposure in the media which we could not have gained purely through advertising in the traditional way."

Sales of Coors have risen dramatically over the past year and Michael is certain a large part of that is due to the Chelsea sponsorship.

"Just the fact that people have seen the brand name before means they are more likely to order it in a bar or buy it in a supermarket or off-licence."

Chelsea's Managing Director Colin Hutchinson saw one

*Message in a bottle. Robin Alexander, Managing Director of Take Home Sales at Scottish Courage Ltd, flanked by Dennis Wise and Glenn Hoddle.*

immediate but unexpected side to the Coors sponsorship.

"Our first batch of shirts featuring the Coors logo sold out just a couple of weeks into the season. That's got to be a good sign. If that's how the shirts are going, the brand won't be far behind!" he said.

"Sponsorship is good for the game but it is important for Chelsea to have the right kind of sponsor and we couldn't have asked for better.

Coors Extra Gold has the right pedigree. It comes from the S&N stable and they have proved that they can operate sponsorships - not only by raising their brands' profile but have excellent relationships with the teams involved.

I wasn't suprised when Robin and other representatives from William Younger came to see us and introduce themselves.

Robin didn't only want to see the players but everyone - right down to the cleaners.

He felt it was important that everyone knew who the new sponsors were and answer any questions anyone might have."

Chelsea manager Glenn Hoddle also recognises the value of a high profile sponsorship tie-up.

"I welcome their positive approach because they are not just going to put money in but take an interest in everything that is happening in the club.

Coors, William Younger and Chelsea make a good team!" he said.

*A new era for the Blues. Chelsea Managing Director Colin Hutchinson signs the sponsorship agreement with Robin Alexander.*

PAUL ELLIOTT'S glittering career as a player may have ended but it has paved the way for a second one.

He is now enjoying life off the field as a radio and TV commentator and a match day host for Coors.

"I am grateful to William Younger and Chelsea for giving me the chance to stay involved with football and the Club," he said.

Paul's playing career was cut cruelly short in 1992 at the age of 28 when he clashed with Liverpool's Dean Saunders at Anfield, severely damaging the ligaments in his right knee.

He had come to Chelsea after spells with Charlton, Luton, Aston Villa, Italian club Pisa and Celtic.

Lewisham-born Paul signed with Charlton Athletic at the age of 16.

He had played football since he was a child with his brothers Geoff, Tony and sister Angela but after unsuccessful trials at West Ham, Luton and Chelsea he was on the verge of giving up his dreams to play professionally when at the age of 15 he was spotted by scout Les Gore when he was playing with friends at Plumstead Common.

"I was beginning to wonder if I had the talent and was really going to concentrate on a career outside football," said Paul.

"I realize now that I was a late developer and am so grateful to Les."

In 1983 he moved to Luton, working with David Pleat, but even then Paul suffered a nasty injury - breaking his leg in two places.

Two years later he transferred to Aston Villa and then in 1987 went to Italy where he was again hit by injury - this time on his right knee.

But the Italian style of football taught him a lot.

"In Italy I learned to play a calculated game and that there was a way to play football with skill as well as power," said Paul.

"It was a great time for me and a very educational one and influenced my style of play at Celtic."

Paul moved to the Glasgow club in 1989, before moving back to London and Chelsea in 1991.

A year later his career was over with an injury described by his surgeon as one of the worst injuries he had ever seen.

"He said it was like a car hitting me while I was stationary," said Paul.

After four operations, Professor David Dandy the leading surgeon in the field and the man who operated on Alan Shearer's knee, told Paul he was able to walk but could not play again.

He had worked so hard to restore his mobility and build up his muscle tone but was faced with no choice.

"I had been injured before and knew what I had to do to ensure my walking and playing was not affected," said Paul.

"It was hard for me. At the age of 28,

*Far left. Paul Elliott in his playing days for Chelsea. Above. Paul taking part in a Coors promotion and, below, showing Coors guests around Stamford Bridge in his role as host, with Ian Copeland, William Younger's commercial director, third from left and Ben Gibson, PR and events manager, fourth from left.*

*William Younger's Managing Director Charles Williamson presents a Man of the Match award to Paul Furlong.*

my footballing career was over. I knew I would have to give up some time but I always expected it to be much later.

I didn't realise what would be in store for me. It was an uncertain time.

If someone had told me that I would still be connected with football the way I am now, I wouldn't have believed them.

It's a great second career. I wish I was still playing, but this is the next best thing."

Paul now works as a commentator for Sky TV and Channel 4 as well as for London's Capital Radio, He is also a scout for Glenn Hoddle and a Matchday Host for William Younger.

As a scout Paul travels all over the country searching out new players for Glenn Hoddle.

"I love it. It's a great chance to look for future talent and a great honour to be asked by Glenn to do it."

A few months ago Paul set up an academy where he lives in Chislehurst, Kent. Twice a week, he coaches 10 and 11 year olds for no money.

"It's my way of giving something back to the game," he said.

His success as a Matchday Host has earned Paul the nickname Mr Hospitality.

William Younger was looking for a host to talk to and entertain their guests when they visited Stamford Bridge for matches.

Ian Copeland, Commercial Director said: "It was important to have the right kind of person to entertain our guests who are in the licensed trade and used to looking after people well.

The sponsorship was a huge commitment to us and it was important that we got it right."

Paul was recommended for the job by Chelsea Managing director Colin Hutchinson.

Colin knew his credentials were perfect for the job - a knowledge of Chelsea from the inside, a friendly manner and pleasing personality.

"At the time, we weren't sure how far the job would develop.

*Right. Ben Gibson welcomes Ruud Gullit to Stamford Bridge on the day he signed for Chelsea.*

But Paul has made it his own," said Ian Copeland,

"He is wonderful with the guests, showing them round the pitch on a tour before the game and entertaining them before and after a match.

He is a natural host - warm, friendly and patient.

*Visiting William Younger's Home Brewery, Nottingham. Back Row, Left-to-right, Charles Williamson, Rosetta Alexander, Robin Alexander, Ken Bates, Suzanne Dwyer, Ian Copeland, Linda Hutchinson, Colin Hutchinson. Seated, Yvonne Todd, Myra Copeland, Dorothy Williamson.*

He never tires of speaking to people and really enjoys it."

So much so, in fact, that William Younger have booked him for personal appearances at many of its pub and club outlets.

"He is a good ambassador for the Club and for Coors,"said Ian.

"We will be booking his services for a long time yet."

Paul summed it up: "I love my role as Matchday Host. Right from the start, I have had a rapport with Coors and William Younger. They are a team of professionals dedicated to getting the sponsorship package right."

## TEN THINGS YOU DIDN'T KNOW ABOUT *Coors*

1. COORS beers are brewed from streams of melted Rocky Mountains snow in Colorado.

2. The yeast used to make COORS EXTRA GOLD is flown from the US to the UK in a business class seat with an American brewer accompanying it on its journey.

3. COORS is the third largest brewer in the USA.

4. UK brewed COORS EXTRA GOLD was named the Best International draught lager in 1994 at the International Brewing Awards.

5. Until 1990 COORS was a regional brewer and fans of COORS EXTRA GOLD used to buy van-loads of beer when they went on holiday to the Colorado area.

6. A new baseball stadium in Denver, Colorado, has been named Coors Field after the brand. It is one of the largest baseball stadiums in the USA.

7. COORS brewery in America is the largest single-site brewery in the world.

8. COORS beers have been brewed in Colorado since 1873. The brewery is still family-run today.

9. There are no added flavourings or preservatives in COORS beers.

10. COORS brewery is named after its founder, Adolph Coors, who emigrated from Prussia in 1868.

KHADIJA BUCKLAND is a writer, designer, publisher, freelance journalist . . . and Chelsea fan.

She formed her publishing company, Red House Publishing, three years ago and has written books on beer and football. She is also a regular contributor to national and regional newspapers and is a member of the British Guild of Beer Writers.